A GUIDE TO 199

MICHIGAN WATERFALLS

Text: Laurie Penrose

Maps: Bill T. Penrose

Black and white photos: Ruth Penrose

Field Coordinator: Bill J. Penrose

Friede Publications

Friede Publications
2339 Venezia Drive
Davison, Michigan 48423

First Printing, May 1988
Second Printing, March 1989
Third Printing, November 1990
Fourth Printing, June 1992
Fifth Printing, September 1993
Sixth Printing, April 1995

Printed in the United States of America

ISBN 0-9608588-7-3

DEDICATION

On May 30, 1934, at Negaunee, Michigan, Grace Anna Hubbert and Joseph Thomas Penrose were wed. Their abiding love has become our legacy, giving us the strength to test the waters of our own imagination. It is to each of them that we dedicate this book.

ACKNOWLEDGMENTS

As with any endeavor of this magnitude, we couldn't have succeeded without the help of many wonderful people. We thank everyone who helped and supported us, especially:

Edmund Hedstrom, park manager, and Tom Proulx, park ranger, at Lake Gogebic State Park, for their assistance in Gogebic County.

Larry Harrington of the Crystal Falls D.N.R. office for his assistance in the Iron County area.

Isabella Sullivan, with the Alger County Historical Society, for her information on the history of the Alger County area.

Grant Petersen, superintendent of the Pictured Rocks National Lakeshore, and his co-workers for their friendly help in the Pictured Rocks area.

Vern and Cora Killinger, West Branch, for their assistance with Spray Falls.

Jim, Todd and Kurt Penrose, Ishpeming, for their help in locating several of the falls in Marquette County.

Kellie Barry-Angeli of the Marquette County Chamber of Commerce for her help in the Marquette-Big Bay area.

Dan Plescher, Baraga State Park manager, for his assistance in the Baraga County area.

Bonny Kinnunen of the Baraga County Area Chamber of Commerce, one of the most informative and cooperative organizations in the U.P. We were very fortunate to find someone as friendly and as giving with time and knowledge as Bonny, and to her we extend a special thanks.

Gary Barfknecht, for his belief in our project and his willingness to follow through on the arduous task of editing and publishing this volume.

Cover photos by Bill J. Penrose

Front cover, clockwise from upper left:

Wagner Falls (p. 20)
Manabezho Falls (p. 132)
Reany Falls (p. 45)
Black River Falls (p. 38)

Back cover: Sable Falls (p. 8)

CONTENTS

APPENDIX I

APPENDIX II

DAM SITES

INTRODUCTION

Michigan's Upper Peninsula is one of the most beautiful areas in the entire country. Throughout it all is the never-ending sound of waves upon the sand, the roar of mighty rivers, and the shy laughter of tiny streams. The voice of the water never leaves you, and it is the underlying theme of this land.

The Upper Peninsula is a special place to our family. My great-grandparents left family and friends and journeyed from England to create a new life over the sea. From the tin mines of Cornwall to the iron mines of Michigan, the focus of our family had shifted. In the years following, many of us moved from the U.P. But no matter how far we go, the area always holds a special place in our hearts.

Some of my strongest memories are of walks in the Upper Peninsula in search of a forgotten spring or a run-down fence-line. No matter how enjoyable walking through the wilderness was, it was always better if you had a destination in mind. For this reason, many years ago we began to seek out the waterfalls of the U.P.

We wrote this book so that others could avoid many of the problems we encountered in our search for waterfalls. Incorrect maps, incomplete directions and unmarked trails were a constant source of irritation. But through hours of research and with the help of some very special people, we eventually found what we were looking for. It is with great pleasure we pass our findings along to you.

From falls you can peer at through your car window to those reachable only after an arduous hike deep into the interior of a forest, there are Michigan waterfalls for everyone. As with us, often your mood will determine what is most appealing, whether it be a long-forgotten pool beneath a gentle falls or the thunder of a river leaping into a gorge.

It's all there waiting for you.

Laurie Penrose
Alger, Michigan

PREFACE

We have made every effort to compose this guidebook in a manner that will make it an enjoyably useful tool. Following are some explanations of our terms and methods.

First, you may wonder why we have bothered to list some waterfalls only to subsequently advise you not to visit them. We have mentioned these falls because they are often included on other waterfall lists, even though in many cases they can't or shouldn't be visited for one or more reasons.

Directions: In the directions to most of the falls, the driving distance is noted in tenths of miles. These numbers may vary somewhat from vehicle to vehicle but should be fairly close.

When you hike to the falls, always take a compass. Though very small, it can suddenly become a large help in the midst of a thick forest. Also, always have a map on hand (U.S. Forest Service maps, a county map book or Michigan D.N.R. maps, for example) for the area you are visiting. Where there are no formal trails to the falls or where the route is complicated, we mark our way in with bright red ribbons, then remove them on the way out.

Private Property: We didn't visit falls that are on private property or where private property had to be crossed to get to them except in those instances when it was possible to obtain permission. We have noted the falls that are on private property, but we did not find out who the landowners are in most cases. If you wish to visit any of those falls, we urge you to find out locally who the landowner is and obtain permission. If this isn't possible, we recommend that you do not visit those falls.

Dams: Several waterfalls throughout the Upper Peninsula have had dams built on top of them, which in most cases elminates the falls. In spite of this, most of these sites are still listed in waterfall directories, even though there are no visible waterfalls. Because of that, plus the fact that many are open to the public for fishing and boating, we have included mention of all dam sites that in the past have been called waterfalls as well as those we know are open to the public.

All dam sites are listed separately at the end of each chapter and are signified by a number followed by the letter *D*.

Upper Tahquamenon Falls (p.4)

—Photo Courtesy of Tom Powers, author of *Natural Michigan*—

CHIPPEWA and LUCE COUNTIES

More than 300 years of history, centered around Sault Ste. Marie, plus natural beauty such as the Hiawatha National Forest and the majestic Tahquamenon Falls combine to make this one of the most interesting and beautiful areas of Michigan.

The first permanent European settlement in Michigan was at Sault Sainte Marie in 1668, and this historic community numbers among the oldest in the United States. During the 17th and 18th centuries, a lively mixture of people passed through and lived in the area as the flags of three different nations were raised over the city's rooftops. French fur traders of the 1600s were among the first to greet the native Americans, and a thriving trade developed. With the rise of British imperialism on the entire continent in the 1700s, England replaced France as the European power in the area. In 1828, 45 years after America won her independence, the last of the British finally left the area, but rugged fur traders were still the mainstay of the area's economy and activity.

But in the mid-1800s everything changed. Industrialism hit Michigan and with a vengeance. Copper and iron ore were discovered in the Upper Peninsula, and commerce there became increasingly important. However, getting the ore to eastern markets cheaply and efficiently via a Great Lakes water route was effectively blocked by the rapids of the St. Mary's River at Sault Ste. Marie. Powerful New York businessmen with interests in the iron and copper industry, however, formulated and carried out a then remarkable plan to solve that problem, and in the process firmly anchored Sault Ste. Marie in the modern age.

In 1855 the first of the "Soo" locks, the engineering and construction marvel of the era, began dropping and raising vessels 22 feet between Lake Superior and Lake Huron. Today, it is the busiest locks system in the world and also boasts the St. Lawrence Seaway's largest lock, which can service monstrous 1000-foot-long ore boats. From their opening, the Soo Locks have attracted millions of visitors, and just about everyone seems to find something fascinating in the wide variety of Great Lakes vessels and foreign ships that pass through the locks daily.   One of the best spots to view the locks is from a beautiful park—with lush landscaped lawns and flower beds nestled beneath shady trees—right next to them. From there you are so close to the huge ships that it seems as though you can reach out and brush their steel sides with your hand.

Looming over the locks to the west is another engineering marvel, the International Bridge, a two-mile-long series of arches and trusses that spans the St. Mary's River to link the United States with Canada. Almost due south of the bridge is Lake Superior State University. The campus, situated atop a hill, occupies the site of Fort Brady, a U.S. Army post established in 1822.

As the St. Mary's River flows southeast from Sault Ste. Marie toward Lake Huron, it courses past dozens of islands, many of which are worth a visit. One short scenic drive, for example, involves taking a ferry to Sugar Island, just east of Sault Ste. Marie. If you have time for a longer trip, take the ferry from De Tour village to Drummond Island, the largest U.S. island on the Great Lakes, and spend the day exploring the site of historic Fort Drummond, the last fort ever manned by British soldiers in the United States.

There are also many museums in the area, and two of particular interest are located in the Tahquamenon Falls area. Inside the Whitefish Point Lighthouse, for example, is the Great Lakes Shipwreck Museum, a collection of artifacts from ships that have sunk in the area. The displays not only vividly show the power of the Great Lakes, but also their hold over the men who sailed upon them. The Tahquamenon Logging Museum, north of Newberry on M-123, on the other hand, provides an opportunity to learn the history of the logging industry in Luce County. By trying out displays set up along the Tahquamenon River, you can easily imagine the frenzied activity of the early loggers as they worked this section of forest.

For further information about Chippewa and Luce counties and their attractions you may contact the following:

Department of Natural Resources
District 4 Office
P.O. Box 445
309 McMillan
Newberry MI 49868

Department of Natural Resources
Newberry Field Office
P.O. Box 445
M-123 South
Newberry MI 49868

Department of Natural Resources
Sault Ste. Marie Field Office
P.O. Box 798
Sault Ste. Marie MI 49783

Drummond Island Chamber of Commerce
Drummond Island MI 49726

Great Lakes Shipwreck Historical Society
Rt. 2, Box 279-A
Sault Ste. Marie MI 49783

Hiawatha Nature and History Association
P.O. Box 246
Rudyard MI 49870

Newberry Area Chamber of Commerce
P.O. Box 308
Newberry MI 49868

Sault Area Chamber of Commerce
2581 I-75 Business Spur
Sault Ste. Marie MI 49783

Upper Peninsula Travel and Recreation
   Association
P.O. Box 400
Iron Mountain MI 49801

U.S. Forest Service
Sault Ste. Marie Ranger District
2901 I-75 Business Spur
Sault Ste. Marie MI 49783

ST. MARY'S RAPIDS

St. Mary's River, Sault Ste. Marie

Early pre-locks photographs of the St. Mary's Rapids show a mass of white water churning roughly over the stones that line the riverbed, the foaming waves punctuated here and there with rocks rising up out of the water. The 3/4-mile-long rapids stretched the width of the river and, in the photos, appear as an unending blur which finally blended into the horizon upstream.

Unfortunately that grandeur was preserved only in photographs. Now only a narrow strip of the rapids flows between the Canadian and American locks at Sault Ste. Marie, and it is difficult to imagine their once-majestic scope.

The rapids that do remain are still impressive but hard to view. The best place to view them is from a Soo Locks tour boat or the Tower of History in downtown Sault Ste. Marie.

There used to be another, though less well-known, rapids in the Sault area. If you take the car ferry from Sault Ste. Marie across the St. Mary's River to Sugar Island, you land on a small outer island separated from the main island by a wide channel. Black Point Rapids used to be located in this channel. We say "used to" because a solid earth causeway—built across the channel as an automobile route between the two islands—effectively cut off the water flow. So today, Black Point Rapids is just a calm, peaceful inlet off the river.

Directions: From I-75, take either of the two business loops and follow the well-marked route to the Soo Locks. In downtown Sault Ste. Marie, turn right (east) onto Portage Street and go .3 miles to the Tower of History, .5 miles to Tour Boat Dock #2 or 1.7 miles to Tour Boat Dock #1.

2

LOWER TAHQUAMENON FALLS

Tahquamenon River, 12 1/2 miles southwest of Paradise

Just before its final 10-mile rush to Whitefish Bay, the wide Tahquamenon River splits around a center island and, at the same time, drops about 20 feet on both sides to form Lower Tahquamenon Falls. The deep copper-colored water splashes over rough sections of large rocks and boulders strewn throughout the river, rejoins at the base of the island, then slips away to the left. For a close-up look at both sections of the falls, take a rental rowboat to the island and walk the trails that circle its edge. You can also view them from lookout points on a high bluff about 100 feet in front of the parking area.

This well-kept area, a small portion of

Michigan's second-largest state park, is ideal for a picnic or even a day-long outing. Facilities include a park store, a playground, and picnic tables and grills set up in a grassy area surrounding the falls.

We also visited the falls in the winter. The road to the parking area was closed, so we had to walk about a mile down a large hill to reach the river. But the snow blanketing the forest created such silent, peaceful surroundings that it was a wonderful walk.

Directions: On M-123 go west from Paradise approximately 12.5 miles to the Lower Tahquamenon Falls State Park, on the left.

3

UPPER TAHQUAMENON FALLS

Tahquamenon River, 15 1/2 miles southwest of Paradise

This is a falls that you don't want to miss. Its enormity (It is the largest falls in Michigan and the second-largest east of the Mississippi.) is spectacular. Golden water rushes over a 200-foot-wide slab of bedrock and drops with a mighty roar 50 feet to the river below. Mists rise up like sentinels and spread into the forest on both sides of the falls. The river here stretches through a deep canyon, and high walls of layered sandstone line the banks. These cliffs are painted with sub-

tle reds and blues, which blend together as they reach the water.

The wide, paved trail which leads from the parking area to the falls forks as it nears the river. The left fork leads to downstream views of the falls; the right fork ends at a viewing area at the top of the falls. This fork follows a ridge 75 feet above the river, and views along the route are sweeping, especially from the several turnoffs. The trail ends at a set of stairs which descend in several levels to a viewing platform at the very crest of the falls. This platform is constructed in such a way that you can view this mighty spectacle nearly head-on.

Tahquamenon Falls is equally beautiful in the winter. Huge ice forms are created above and behind the sheet of falling water, and spires of ice reach up to meet the flow from the frozen river below. Icicles, created by water running from small streams over and between the rocks, decorate the canyon's stone walls. Mixed with the colored stone, the icicles take on a delicate blue tint, which highlights their sparkling beauty.

Facilities at this well-maintained state park include benches along the trails, drinking fountains and restrooms.

Directions: From M-123 go west from Paradise approximately 15.5 miles to signs on the left which point the way to the Upper Falls. The Lower Tahquamenon Falls are located three miles east on M-123.   (Photo, p. *xiv*)

ALGER COUNTY

If you travel west across the Upper Peninsula, Alger County is the first with numerous waterfalls to visit. Many other natural wonders lie within the borders of this irregularly shaped parcel of land which borders Lake Superior in the north-central U.P. An added plus: large areas of state and federal land are open to the public throughout the county, including 70,000 acres administered by the National Park Service in the Pictured Rocks National Lakeshore.

That impressive scenic area stretches from Munising to Grand Marais and includes nearly 40 miles of breathtaking Lake Superior shoreline. You can experience an almost overwhelming solitude there, whether you sit beside cascading water, walk along the beaches in search of agates or watch the sun set across the vast expanse of Lake Superior. You can also absorb history. The Pictured Rocks area is the setting for many of the legends of Hiawatha, and as you stroll along the shore of Lake Superior, you are often following routes used by Ojibway Indians more than 100 years ago. Their paths are among miles of beautiful hiking trails which lead to waterfalls and other scenic areas throughout the park.

But the Pictured Rocks themselves—which stretch from just north of Munising for 15 miles northeast along Lake Superior—are the park's most prominent feature. You can glimpse the rocks from shore, but for the best views, take the boat tour, which begins in Munising. A few miles from town, the rocky shoreline begins to rise until it forms huge towering sandstone cliffs. The most unusual of these formations have been given names such as Miners Castle and Chapel Rock.

Past the Pictured Rocks are the Grand Sable Banks, huge cliffs of dark reddish-brown sand which fall steeply to meet the blue waters of Lake Superior. From these banks eastward toward Grand Marais is one of the best agate beaches in the Upper Peninsula.

Offshore from these beaches and stretching from Au Train Point to the Au Sable Point area is another unique park, an underwater diving preserve. The natural deep-water harbors of both Munising and Grand Marais have long attracted ships seeking shelter from raging Lake Superior storms. Many Great Lakes vessels, however, fell prey to their fury, and the lake bottom along all of Alger County's shoreline is littered with wrecks. The underwater preserve was established to allow diving while protecting those wrecks from pilfering. Several businesses in the area not only rent diving equipment, but also offer lessons and charters. Non-divers can view the hulls of several sunken ships from the shoreline. Just follow the beach from Hurricane River eastward until you reach Au Sable Lighthouse. Along this stretch are the remains of many sunken ships, either a few feet under the water or sometimes partially buried in the beach itself.

The two cities that serve as the gateways to this unique area are also worth a visit. On the east is Grand Marais, a peaceful, picturesque village which rests on the shore of Lake Superior. On the west is Munising, which is bounded on the north by Lake Superior and enclosed on its other three sides by very high hills and ridges. That terrain is a natural location for waterfalls, and many are located either in the city itself or in the surrounding area.

For more specific information on Alger County and its attractions, you may contact:

Alger County Historical Society
203 W. Onota St.
Munising MI 49862

Grand Marais Chamber of Commerce
Grand Marais MI 49839

Hiawatha National Forest Headquarters
2727 N. Lincoln Rd.
Escanaba MI 49829

Michigan Nature Association
7981 Beard Rd.
P.O. Box 102
Avoca MI 48006

U.S. Forest Service
Rapid River MI 49878

National Park Service
Pictured Rocks National Lakeshore
Munising MI 49862

4

CHIPMUNK FALLS

Chipmunk Creek, 1 1/2 miles east of Grand Marais

According to local residents, not only do these falls run mainly only in the spring or after heavy rains, but also they are on private property and not open to the public.

5

SABLE FALLS

Sable Creek, 1 1/2 miles west of Grand Marais

Located just west of Grand Marais, Sable Falls marks the east border of the Pictured Rocks National Lakeshore. The falls drops through a deep valley the river has carved into the surrounding sand and heavy underlying bedrock, and high sand cliffs border the flow on both sides. Though relatively small, Sable Falls is nevertheless dramatic as it courses over large boulders strewn in its path.

The quarter-mile path to the falls from a parking lot about a mile west of Grand Marais is smooth, wide and very easy going. At the falls itself, an extensive stairway system drops to another path, to the right of the river, which leads to one of the best agate beaches in Michigan.

An alternate route (and a good afternoon excursion) is to park in the Grand Marais Municipal parking lot and walk west down the beach about a mile, until you reach the mouth of Sable Creek. From there, you can walk less than a quarter of a mile to the falls, or continue down the shore along the Grand Sable Banks, a majestic sight you won't want to miss. You can also get to the banks by driving west on H-58 to Grand Sable Lake, with opportunities for swimming and fishing, plus a chance to scale the huge dunes that brush up against the lake's north shore.

Directions: Go west out of Grand Marais on H-58 for about one mile to a parking lot, on the right, and the start of the trail to Sable Falls.

SPRAY FALLS

Spray Creek, 6 1/2 miles north of Melstrand

The isolation and powerful beauty of this falls make it one of the most enjoyable in the area. Spray Creek—a small stream which winds its way through the birches, hemlock and mountain ash of the surrounding forest—finally bursts free of its confines and dramatically plunges nearly 70 feet directly into the sparkling blue waters of Lake Superior.

Directions: Drive approximately five miles east of Melstrand on H-58 to Beaver Lake Road. Turn left (north) onto Beaver Lake Road and go approximately three miles to a parking area on the left (before you reach Little Beaver Lake Campgrounds). It is about a three-mile walk to Spray Falls from this parking area. (The trail to Spray Falls is part of a network of trails in the Pictured Rocks National Lakeshore, and since there are several converging trails in the area, we advise that you pick up a trail map from one of the two visitors centers located near both park entrances.)

Take the right loop of the White Pine Trail, which leads past both Beaver Lake and Little Beaver Lake. Small, shallow "sea caves"—hollows in the rock ledge carved by the pounding of the lake thousands of years ago—border the inside of sections of this trail. After about a mile, at Lake Superior, the White Pine Trail intersects the Lakeshore Trail. (This trail runs the length of the national lakeshore, along the rim of the Pictured Rocks, and offers some spectacular views of the multi-colored cliffs and the deep blue-greens of the lake.) Turn left and walk west along the Lakeshore Trail for about

two miles to Spray Falls. There are no signs announcing it, so keep alert for the sounds of the falls splashing into the lake far below when you approach the area. A wooden bridge spans Spray Creek, but since the falls faces Lake Superior, you must view it from any area of the trail that extends farther out into the lake before the trail reaches the small stream.

Alger County

7

CHAPEL FALLS

Section Creek, 5 1/2 miles north of Melstrand

You can get to both Chapel and Mosquito falls (#9) from the same parking area, and if you have time, you should visit both. Chapel Falls, which is more popular, is dramatic, whereas Mosquito Falls is secluded and personal.

The 1.3-mile trail to Chapel Falls, though steep at times, is actually more like a road. It is very wide, and even further improvements were being made when we visited in the fall of 1986. As you approach the river, the path skirts a ridge, and through the trees you can glimpse the sweeping vista of rolling hills that surround Chapel Lake far below.

To view the falls you must cross Section Creek, which is easily accomplished on a small bridge built by the park service. Once across, a 100-yard-long foot trail leads to a clearing on a bluff (a perfect spot for a picnic) with a riveting view

of the falls and tree-covered canyon. Framed by pine boughs, white spray hurls itself over the cliff, passes briefly over the black rock, then gathers its forces to rush through an opening in the trees. This falls is aptly named, for the panorama inspires a powerful sense of serenity.

If you like to hike, you can continue from the falls on a trail which circles Chapel Lake, then heads toward Lake Superior. Although we didn't try it, that day-long walk is both beautiful and very popular, according to park service personnel.

Directions: From H–58 just north of Melstrand turn left onto a gravel road marked by a Chapel Falls sign and continue to follow the signs about six miles to the Chapel Falls parking area.

8

UNNAMED FALLS

Chapel Creek, 4 miles northwest of Melstrand

Just south of the Chapel Falls parking area, a small stream slips beneath the roadway and flows west to Chapel Creek and an unnamed falls. The absence of a well-worn trail to the falls makes for rough going over a few spots and also sets up the possibility of getting lost. But if you stay close to the flowing water, you shouldn't have any problem. As you fol-

low its left bank, the small creek makes several one-foot drops over smooth stone shelves. The banks rise until, about 100 yards from the road, you look down on the stream's junction with Chapel Creek from a height of about 12 feet.

From the junction, go left, up Chapel Creek, about 50 yards to the falls. You will approach the falls on a high cliff,

Chapel Lake

CHAPEL FALLS

MOSQUITO
FALLS

UNNAMED
FALLS

Parking Area

N

Miles

0   1/2   1

H-58

H-58

Melstrand

with steep sides to the canyon below, so use extreme care. The falls themselves consist of a 200-foot-long series of drops, the highest falling about 30 feet into the steep canyon below. From the top of the ridge, you can only glimpse this falls in sections.

To get a better view, you would have to walk in the canyon itself, that is, remain on the banks of both the unnamed creek and Chapel Creek. That would not be easy, however. The banks of both streams are sometimes steep, which would require some difficult maneuvering.

Directions: From H-58 just north of Melstrand turn left onto a gravel road marked by a Chapel Falls sign and continue to follow the signs about six miles to the Chapel Falls parking area. As you approach the parking lot you will cross a small stream. After parking your car, walk back down the road, cross the stream, then turn right and follow the stream as noted in the text.

MOSQUITO FALLS

Mosquito River, 5 miles northwest of Melstrand

Though somewhat small and unimposing, Mosquito Falls is very accessible and charming in a quaint way. The Mosquito River here slides, then cascades over layers and shelves of black rock, leaving small pools in its wake. You can wade in the water, and the ledges are a perfect place to sit and soak under the spray. A faint trail to the right, along the riverbank, follows this small falls as it continues another 150 to 200 feet.

Chapel Falls (#7) is located only about two and a half miles from Mosquito Falls, and if you have time, you should visit both.

Directions: From H-58 just north of Melstrand turn left onto a gravel road marked by a Chapel Falls sign and continue to follow the signs about six miles to the Chapel Falls parking area. Leave your vehicle and walk back up the road that you came in on about 200 yards to the second trail on your right. Go about 200 yards on this unimproved logging road, down a short but steep hill and across Chapel Creek. After you cross the stream, it's an easy 1.2-mile walk to the falls. (Map, p. 11)

10

BRIDAL VEIL FALLS

8 miles northeast of Munising

Silvery white tendrils of water fan out over the cliffs of the Pictured Rocks and slide 100 feet down to meet the world's largest freshwater lake. And as they run down the smooth, multicolored stone, they form the reason for the falls name— an outline remindful of a bride's veil.

For the easiest, though distant, views of Bridal Veil Falls, look northeast from the observation platform high atop the rock formation called Miner's Castle. Avid hikers can get closer by walking approximately two miles along the Lakeshore Trail from Miners Castle. (We do not recommend this hike for the average tourist, however, because of the dangerous cliffs in the area.) The best way to view the falls is to take the boat tour out of Munising.

This falls is usually only a spring runner, but we were lucky enough to see it after a heavy summer rainfall.

Directions: To get to Miners Castle, go east on H-58 from Munising approximately 4.5 miles to Miners Castle Road. Turn north onto Miners Castle Road and go about five miles to its end.

(Map, p. 14)

MINERS FALLS

Miners River, 6 miles northeast of Munising

A clearly marked, wide, smooth path—which curves for half a mile through tall, stately hardwoods—leads to one of the most popular waterfalls in the Pictured Rocks National Lakeshore. To view the falls, however, you must descend an extensive stairway which becomes a fairly strenuous climb as you leave. When you reach the viewing platform at the bottom, you can settle back in one among the row of seats and contemplate the falls.

The Miners River here spills out of the forest, then drops 30 to 40 feet in a forceful stream of white spray. Behind the flow, a small hollow has formed in the face of the cliff. The force of the water has worn other round holes in the bedrock at the base of the falls to create some interesting patterns and compositions in the stone's surface.

When you visit Miners Falls, we would highly recommended a side trip to Miners Castle, north of the falls. From this nine-story-tall monolithic rock, you get a breathtaking view of the Pictured Rocks and the blue-green waters of Lake Superior directly below. RV parking is available there as well as restrooms (open during the summer months) with facilities for the handicapped. For directions to Miners Castle, see Bridal Veil Falls (# 10).

Directions: On H-58 drive east from Munising approximately 4.5 miles to Miners Castle Road. Turn left (north) onto Miners Castle Road and go about three and a half miles o a road marked by a "Miners Falls" sign. Turn right (east) and follow this road to the Miners Falls parking area and the start of the trail to the falls. (Map, p. 14)

MUNISING FALLS

Munising

Just inside the eastern limits of the city of Munising, a paved path through the woods which lines Munising Creek leads to a unique opportunity. Not only can you *see* Munising Falls, but because of the large overhang of bedrock that creates them, you can actually pass *behind* them without getting wet.

The five-minute walk from the Pictured Rocks National Lakeshore Visitors Center leads first to a platform and some excellent views of the "pride of Munising."

The falls drops a sheer 40–50 feet into a canyon of multicolored rocks. Rosy hues mix with earth browns and golds to frame the water with color.

From the viewing platform, you can continue on a sandy path under the ledge over which the falls drops and stand behind them. Experiencing the powerful energy of the water rushing by in front of you within arm's reach is exhilarating.

(Continued on p. 14)

MUNISING FALLS
(Continued from p. 13)

Munising Falls is just as beautiful in the winter. The motion of its cascades is frozen like a stop-action picture, with a huge apparently solid pillar of ice that stretches the entire height of the falls. But if you move close enough you can catch a glimpse of water still falling beneath the frozen shell. Rarely will you get the chance to see such a beautiful, majestic sight with so little effort. The path to the falls is kept clear, and to our surprise even the visitors center restrooms were open during our winter visit.

During the summer the building is alive with activity, including interpretive programs. Maps of the Pictured Rocks Na-

tional Lakeshore are displayed, and pleasant, informative park personnel can answer any questions you might have about the area. There's plenty of room for RVs in the parking lot, and a wheelchair is available at the front desk for handicapped visitors.

Directions: From M-28 where it makes a 90-degree turn in Munising, go east on H-58 (Munising Avenue) about a mile and a quarter to Washington Street, on the left. Turn left (north) onto Washington Street and go a little more than a half mile to where it bears right, at a hospital. The Munising Falls parking area is located across the street from the hospital. (You can, in fact, use the hospital signs along the route to direct you to the falls.)

END OF FALLS IN THE PICTURED ROCKS

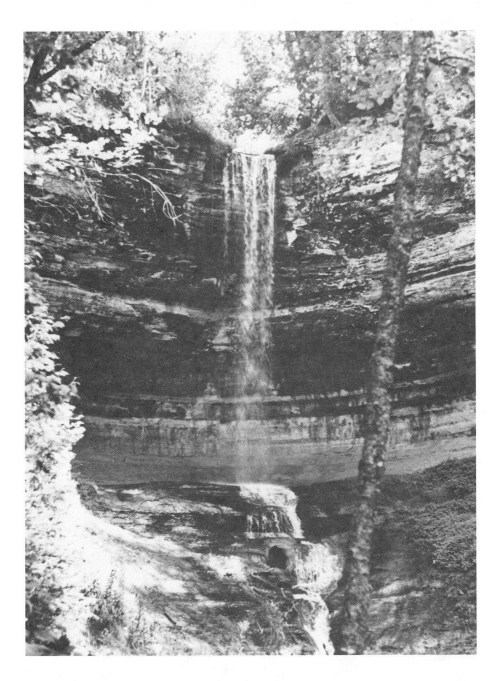

Munising Falls

13

MEMORIAL FALLS
Unnamed Creek, Munising

A short, easy trail leads to the edge of a deep canyon where a three-foot-wide stream plunges over the lip, hits a rock ledge, then continues its 30-foot drop to the sandy floor below. Tall sandstone walls—which extend downstream and out of sight—seem to stand guard over this delicate falls. The rock walls on both sides of the stream are deeply undercut, even behind the falls itself, which creates an area of deep shadows behind strands of sparkling water. Tall pines and hardwoods blanket the top of the rocky ridges to the very edge, where their roots snake down the surface of the rock.

Memorial Falls is a recent addition to the list of Alger County falls. It has been around for millions of years, of course, but was not open to the public until 1987.

At that time it became part of a public nature preserve opened by the Michigan Nature Association, which had purchased land surrounding this falls as well as nearby Tannery Falls.

Directions: From M-28 where it makes a 90-degree turn in Munising, go east on H-58 (Munising Avenue) about a mile and a half to Nestor Street, on the right. Turn right (south) onto Nestor Street and go about one block to signs on the right, which mark the trails to Memorial Falls.

Several paths through this beautiful natural area lead to the falls. Because of the fragile nature of the area, please stay on the existing trails. Also, since you approach Memorial Falls from the top of the canyon, use extreme care.

(Map, p.14)

14

TANNERY FALLS
(Also called Rudy M. Olson Memorial Falls)

Tannery Creek, Munising

The walk to Tannery Falls (renamed Rudy M. Olson Memorial Falls) is as beautiful as the falls themselves. The layered patterns in the surrounding soft sandstone are exquisite, and the trail affords a closeup view of their golden rose colors.

As the trail approaches the falls, the canyon walls rise upward, curve toward the center and extend slightly over the

trail. The sensation is much like being inside an inverted bowl whose base has been removed. A mound of debris—dirt and stones that have fallen from the sides of the cliff—have piled up to fill a portion of the bowl in front of the falls. Narrow Tannery Creek flows over the side of the sandstone layers, fans out across the mossy steps, then falls 40 feet directly to the floor of the canyon below. There, the

Tannery Falls

white tendrils of water rejoin, and the stream cuts to the right and grazes the sandstone wall as it continues on its course. Tannery Falls has always been a beautiful falls but, under private ownership, was closed to the public for many years. Thanks to the Michigan Nature Association—which purchased the land surrounding Tannery Falls and created a public nature preserve, which also includes nearby Memorial Falls—it is open to the public once again.

Directions: From M-28 where it makes a 90-degree turn in Munising, go east on H-58 (Munising Avenue) about a mile and a quarter to the intersection with Washington Street, on the left. Just past that intersection, park on the right (south) side of H-58 across from a short blacktop road on the left that joins H-58 and Washington Street. The trail to the falls begins directly across H-58 from that connecting road.

We were advised to approach the falls on a trail behind an abandoned house just to the north of the trailhead and river. That trail, however, was a mucky quagmire most of the way. The trail on the south side of the river, on the other hand, is easy walking on high ground all the way to the falls. (Map, p. 14)

HORSESHOE FALLS

Stutts Creek, Munising

Located inside the city limits of Munising, Horseshoe Falls is so accessible that it shouldn't be missed. An added attraction: some entertainment for children, who may become bored on long hikes to some of the other falls in the area.

Horseshoe Falls is privately owned, and you have to pass through a small gift shop, plus pay a small fee to view them. Outside the gift shop, a fence encloses a trout pond, where the kids (or you) can feed the fish. A paved walkway meanders through a small botanical garden, and a trail to the right leads less than 100 feet to the falls.

The falls itself is small, with a stream falling about 10 feet over the lip of a bowl. The water then bubbles around a few boulders and continues on its way under some small foot bridges. A hollow, which cuts deeply into the face of the cliff, originally gave the falls a very distinct horseshoe shape. But with the passing of time, falling rocks and earth have changed the contour of the rock walls, and the original shape is no longer well-defined.

Directions: From M-28 near Munising's southern limits (about one-half mile north of Alger Falls), turn east onto Prospect Street. Go approximately two blocks to Bell Avenue and turn left (north). Go approximately one block to the Horseshoe Falls parking area and gift shop, on the right.

16

ALGER FALLS

Alger Creek, 1 mile south of Munising

Just a few yards from M-28 a small outcropping of rocks emerge from the surrounding hillside, and water spills over them in a series of cascades. Despite its proximity to the highway, the serenity of this falls prevails as it drops through a small, almost overlooked valley.

It couldn't be any easier to view Alger Falls. Just pull your vehicle off the highway and study its simple beauty through the window if you like. However, for more intimate views or better camera angles, walk about 30 feet closer to the river.

Directions: From Munising go south on M-28 approximately one mile to where M-94 branches off to the right (west). Alger Falls is on the left (east) side of M-28 at this point.

N

M-28

LAKE SUPERIOR

H-58

Munising

HORSESHOE FALLS

Miles

0   1/2   1

ALGER FALLS

M-94

WAGNER
FALLS

M-28/M-94

Wetmore

Alger County

19

WAGNER FALLS

Wagner Creek, 1 1/2 miles south of Munising

A substantial volume of water confined to a relatively small space makes Wagner Falls a roaring, powerful example of one of Michigan's small waterfalls. The falls is narrow but deep, and the water slides over several heavy rock ledges. Large rocks divide the stream, and several fallen trees bridge the sides of the falls.

Wagner Falls, located within easy driving distance of Alger Falls (#16), was donated to the people of the State of Michigan by the Michigan Division of the Women's Farm and Garden Association Inc.

Directions: From Munising go south on M-28 approximately one mile to where M-94 branches off to the right (west). Turn right (west) onto M-94 and go approximately a half mile to a small roadside area (marked by a Wagner Falls sign) on the left (south).

The path to the falls is only about 300 yards long, but it tends to be swampy for the first 20 yards. After that, wooden walkways cover the muddy sections of the trail. We visited on a rainy afternoon, and the walkways were slippery. But the path quickly climbed, then ran through a forest of translucent greens and golden fall colors. (Map, p.19)

SCOTT FALLS

8 miles northwest of Munising

Scott Falls is close enough to M-28 to view from your car. However, it is such a charming falls, we suggest that you get close enough to feel the water with your hands.

A medium-size stream of water drops about 10 feet directly into a small pool lined with sand and small pebbles. The rock shelf behind the stream has been hollowed out, so it is possible to walk behind the falls and hold out your hand to catch the strong rush of water.

Scott Falls is not only a fun, popular break for automobile travelers, but also can be a stopover for snowmobilers. In the winter its heavy stream forms a beautiful column of ice. The cave behind the frozen pillar is covered with an icy carpet, and large icicles decorate the walls.

Directions: Scott Falls is located on the south side of M-28 just east of H.J. Rathfoot State Roadside Park, approximately two miles east of Au Train.

(Photo, p. 27)

19

SILVER BELL FALLS
Nelson Creek, 7 1/2 miles northwest of Chatham

Silver Bell Falls (sometimes called Silver Falls) is small, humbly beginning from tiny Nelson Creek, but it drops about 30 feet over the dark, layered side of a steep cliff in the middle of the woods. As the water falls down the side of the soft mossy wall, it widens to about 10 feet. Viewed from either side the falls is beautiful in its simplicity. It is especially nice in the spring or after a heavy rain, when the creek, and thus the falls, swells in size.

Before or after your visit to Silver Bell Falls, we recommend a trip to Rock River Falls (#20). The two are very close together and are good comparisons of the diversity of Michigan waterfalls.

Directions: From M-94 where it makes a 90-degree bend in Chatham, turn north onto Rock River Road. Go 3.5 miles, cross the the Rock River, then go another .1 miles to USFS-2276. This road is narrow and rocky but in good condition. Turn left (west) onto USFS-2276 and go approximately 3.6 miles to where it jogs sharply left. Continue straight for .9 miles to an iron gate which crosses the road.

The mile walk to the falls begins at that gate. After 10 minutes of walking, the road forks; follow the right fork straight ahead, past a small parking area on the right to where the road turns into a trail. Continue straight ahead on this trail over a culvert, at about 50 yards, to the falls, about 50 feet farther, on the right.

20

ROCK RIVER FALLS
Rock River, 5 miles northwest of Chatham

A 20-foot drop in the Rock River near Chatham has created one of the most beautiful, secluded falls in Alger County. And though the falls are still remote, extensive work done by the U.S. Forest Service has made it much easier to reach them than in the past.

As we traveled the path to the falls, we noticed a large abandoned sled at the side of the trail. When we walked closer, we could see that it was an old logging sled, with trees growing through it that were at least 20 years old. It was strange to see a remnant of civilization in such a remote location, but it reminded us that we were not the first to travel this way, nor would we be the last.

After a half-hour walk through thick, beautiful woods, we reached the river about 30 yards above the falls. The river

(Continued on p. 23)

ROCK RIVER FALLS
(Continued from p. 22)

here is divided into two streams by a dry rocky area, which traps the autumn leaves. The water slides out of the woods under fallen trees and past rocky banks, then drops about 20 feet down the side of a rock ledge. The water catches on the steps of the ledge, creating progressively smaller streams which form feathery trails from top to bottom. The best view of the falls comes from directly in front of it.

At the base of the falls is a large, dark and apparently still pool. Those adventurous enough to wade, however, will discover that the hidden current of the river pulls through it.

While in the area we met a native, who recommended a cross-country ski trip from Rumely (a small town four miles southwest of the falls) to the valley which surrounds the river and falls. The man, a forest-service employee, said it is a particularly beautiful trip because ice caves—walls of ice created when water seeps out of the side of the rock and freezes—line the valley in the winter.

Before or after your visit to Rock River falls, we recommend a trip to Silver Bell Falls. The two are very close together and are good comparisons of the diversity of Michigan waterfalls.

Directions: From M-94 where it makes a 90-degree bend in Chatham, turn north onto Rock River Road. Go 3.5 miles, cross the Rock River, then go another .1 mile to USFS-2276. This road is narrow and rocky but in good condition. Turn left (west) onto USFS-2276 and go approximately 4.3 miles (it jogs sharply left at 3.6 miles) to a small parking area on the left marked by a sign pointing the way to the trail to Rock River Falls. The 3/4-mile path is mostly downhill, and the ground becomes wet as you reach the bottom.

AU TRAIN FALLS

Au Train River, 10 miles southwest of Munising

On the left as you descend to the falls from the parking area, small trickles of water continuously run over and down rock walls, which are covered by a thick layer of moss in some areas. This unusual smooth cliff was carved out of the heavy stone shelf by the local power company as they cut the short but steep access road to the falls.

At the bottom, as you turn and look back up, you realize that the trees on the right side of the path were hiding something. The river sweeps out of the forest in a thin layer of sparkling water which carpets smooth rock shelves. A bridge, also built by the power company, effectively breaks the panorama of the falls in half. Even so, the view is sweeping. The level of the 60-foot-wide river drops in a series of short cascades and tumbling water, then slides under the steel bridge.

Below the bridge, the river runs much the same, with the addition of a few small natural fishing and wading pools. The pools look inviting, but be sure of your footing if you wade. The shallow water and smooth rocks make for ideal growth conditions for slippery moss and algae.

Directions: From the junction of M-28/ M-94 south of Munising, go west on M-94 approximately 12.5 miles to the village of Forest Lake. Approximately a quarter of a mile west of town, turn right (north) onto USFS-2278, the first road past the Au Train River. On USFS-2278, cross the railroad tracks, then turn right (east) onto the first gravel road (marked with an "Au Train Falls" sign). The parking area is at the end of this road, and the trail to the falls starts at the iron gate.

Alger County

LAUGHING WHITEFISH FALLS

Laughing Whitefish River, 2 1/2 miles northeast of Sundell

Laughing Whitefish Falls' spectacular 100-foot drop, plus its deep gorge and layered limestone walls make it one of the most beautiful in Alger County. As you gaze up from its base at the huge wall of sparkling, shimmering rock, it's hard to believe that it all comes from just one small stream.

No large rushes of water pour over the face of the rock. The water's movement is traced only by a general dampness in shaded areas and a blinding brilliance in the sunlit sections. (The reflections off the water make it difficult to take photographs when the sun is directly overhead which, unfortunately, is when the falls is most spectacular.) The stream continues along the layered limestone and catches in a small pool, and only the twinkling of the water betrays its movement as it runs its course unaffected by the falls it has just left behind.

The 20-minute walk to the falls is mostly downhill through a lovely hardwood forest. The trail begins as a well-kept woodchip-covered path through a meadow filled with berry bushes and tall grasses. Wildflowers peek out through the clumps of bushes and young trees until the trail cuts through a thickly wooded area about a half mile to an extensive flight of stairs. The falls doesn't announce itself with a roar of water or any sudden, sweeping vistas, and it comes as almost a surprise when you reach the top of the stairs.

As you climb or descend the stairs, you can rub your hands along the shallow depressions and caves that line the rim of the canyon. Also from the stairs you can see small streams as they wind their way through the undergrowth to the base of the falls.

Directions: From M-94 in Sundell, turn north at a Michigan scenic-site sign and go approximately two miles to a gravel road (also marked with a scenic-site sign). Turn right (east) and follow this road approximately a half mile to the Laughing Whitefish Falls parking area.

WHITEFISH FALLS

Whitefish River, 5 miles northwest of Trenary

Whitefish Falls is actually a series of three drops spaced at about 50-yard intervals. The first falls comes into distant view early in the short walk to them. As you get closer you see that, across the entire width of the river, the water drops about four feet and becomes copper-colored as it rushes over the bedrock slabs. Farther upstream the second and third falls, each with a drop of about a foot, form twin copper bands which span the river.

The trail to the falls is only about 150 yards long, but it is a lovely walk along the banks of a beautiful river. Huge cedars and hardwoods bend out over the water from the large limestone slabs which border both sides. The stone "carpet" provides a very easy path to follow, and it also is a good place to sit and soak your feet in the swift current.

Directions: From the intersection of M-67 and US-41 (approximately three quarters of a mile west of Trenary on M-67 and about 18 miles north of Rapid River on US-41), go north on US-41 approximately 3.5 miles and turn left onto the first gravel road past Diffin Road, on the left. This fairly wide, well-maintained trail road loops back to US-41 about a quarter of a mile north, so you don't have to turn your vehicle around to leave. As you reach the point where the loop is farthest from US-41, you will be able to hear the river. Park in this area, walk down the bank to the river, and head upstream.

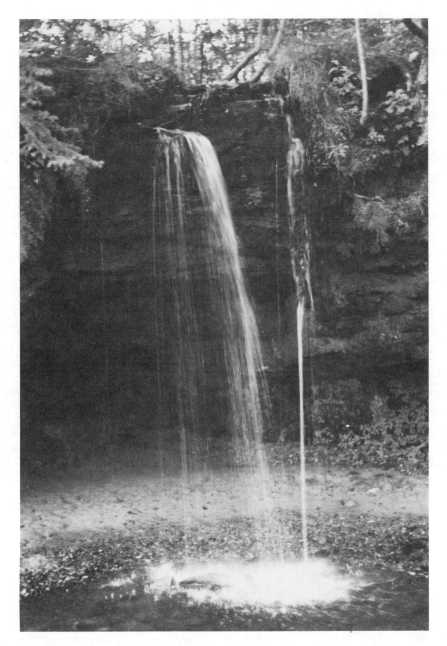

Scott Falls (p. 21)

MARQUETTE COUNTY

Reany Falls (p. 45)

Marquette County, Michigan's largest, is truly a vacationer's paradise. Its borders enclose more lakes, 835, than any other Michigan county, and its more than 1,000,000 acres of land is networked with hundreds of miles of snowmobile, hiking and cross-country ski trails. Downhill skiers, too, have many areas to choose from, and skiers and non-skiers alike will enjoy a visit to the National Ski Hall of Fame in Ishpeming.

The city of Marquette, home of Northern Michigan University, is the center of the county's activity. The iron-ore industry first opened up this area, and you can still watch ore being loaded onto huge Great Lakes ships at the world's first pocket ore dock. But Marquette now has many other industries, as well as a beautifully restored downtown business district built along the hillsides bordering Lake Superior.

The lake, in fact, has become the focal point of the city, and one of the most beautiful of the many attractions lining its shore is Presque Isle Park. A paved roadway skirts this small island, and several platforms along the route provide some outstanding vistas of Lake Superior. The views from the huge cliffs are especially spectacular during high winds, when tremendously powerful waves crash against the sides of the deep-brown rocks. Many families also cross the narrow strip of land which connects this day park to Marquette to enjoy a variety of man-made attractions, including a waterslide, a marina, picnic facilities and a small zoo.

A few miles west of Marquette, Negaunee (site of Michigan's first iron-ore discovery) and Ishpeming lie in the center of the Marquette Iron Range. The area's shaft mines have all closed, but there are a few open-pit mines still in operation. The Empire Mine, in Palmer, is the most active, and you can view the Tilden Mine, south of Negaunee, from a public overlook. The Michigan Iron Industry Museum in Negaunee is the most recent addition to several interesting museums in the area.

Just west of Negaunee and Ishpeming is six-mile-long Lake Michigamme, whose golden waters and many small islands are very popular with boaters, fishermen and swimmers. Just north of that area, a total of 59 moose were transplanted from Canada by the Michigan DNR in an attempt to re-establish a herd in the Huron Mountains.

Numerous waterfalls are scattered throughout Marquette County. Most, unfortunately, are located on private property. Those open to the public, however, present a wide variety, with accessibility ranging from easy, short walks to strenuous hikes into some of the most rugged, untouched areas of the Upper Peninsula.

For more specific information about Marquette County and its attractions you may contact the following:

Department of Natural Resources
District 1 Office
P.O. Box 190, US-41 South
Marquette MI 49855

Department of Natural Resources
Gwinn Field Office
P.O. Box 800
Gwinn MI 49841

Department of Natural Resources
Ishpeming Field Office
632 Teal Lake Rd.
Ishpeming MI 49849

Department of Natural Resources
110 Ford Rd.
Marquette MI 49855

Greater Ishpeming Chamber of Commerce
661 Palms Ave.
Ishpeming MI 49849

Marquette Area Chamber of Commerce
501 S. Front St.
Marquette MI 49855

Michigamme Lakes Country Association
Box 17
Michigamme MI 49861

Marquette County Historical Society
213 N. Front St.
Marquette MI 49855

Upper Peninsula Travel and Recreation
    Association
P.O. Box 400
Iron Mountain MI 49801

24

UPPER FALLS

Chocolay River, 2 1/2 miles northwest of Carlshend

The falls is located on private property.

25

FROHLING FALLS
(Also known as Chocolay Falls)

West Branch Chocolay River, 8 miles northeast of Gwinn

This falls is located on private property.

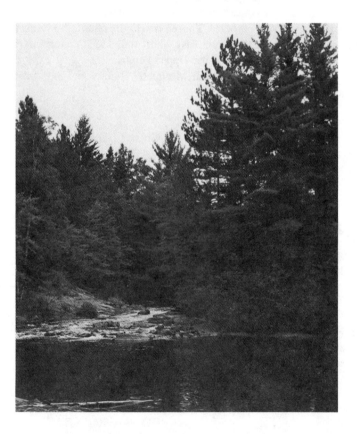

Second Falls, East Branch Escanaba River

Marquette County

26

FIRST FALLS

27

SECOND FALLS

East Branch Escanaba River, Gwinn

The East Branch of the Escanaba River makes two small drops as it flows through a lovely area at a tourist park in Gwinn.

There is a swimming area at the base of the First Falls and a beach along the riverbank. The falls drops only about two feet through a low section of stone which spans the wide river, and its ripples are quickly swallowed up by the stillness of the pond.

A small walking trail, which follows the slow-moving river as it disappears around a bend, leads upstream about a quarter of a mile to another small falls. As you look upstream to a sharp right turn, you can see the small falls cradled in the bend. This falls, too, drops not more than two feet over an isolated section of stone. The river then quickly recovers and becomes as smooth as glass once again. The immense size of the pines that line the opposite bank, their limbs extending over the river, exaggerate the smallness of this falls.

Directions: From M-35 in Gwinn turn north at a blinker light onto Iron Street and go about three blocks to the Gwinn Tourist Park, in a large fenced-in area on the left. The trail to the falls goes upstream from a beach area on the right.

28

TIGER FALLS

Schweitzer Creek, 2 1/2 miles southeast of Palmer

This falls, off Co. Rd. ML, is on private property.

29

SCHWEITZER FALLS

Schweitzer Creek, 2 miles south of Palmer

Near Palmer, Schweitzer Creek drops some 30–35 feet in two distinct stages to form Schweitzer Falls. Tucked under the spreading branches of maple and pine which grow from the right bank, the upper falls separates into two streams as it drops about 20 feet. A large flow on the left foams down the black rock, and a small stream on the right feathers out over the shaded stone. At the base of this upper falls they rejoin to form a small pool.

From there, the stream then quickly reaches the lower falls, where it suddenly plunges 10 feet, slides across a table of smooth black rock, then drops an additional four feet over a scattering of small rocks. A pool at its base casts the reflection of a towering section of smooth, rounded red stone which forms the left bank. A second falls, which can't be seen, creates a disturbance in the surface of this pool on the far side of the rock. The riverbed downstream is littered with small rocks and fallen logs, and as the creek washes over them, the sun reflects off the sparkling surface of the water.

Directions: From M-35 south of Palmer (just past a Standard gas station on the right) turn right (west) onto Co. Rd. 476 and go about 1.2 miles to Co. Rd. 565. Turn left (south) onto Co. Rd. 565 and go approximately 1.1 miles to a

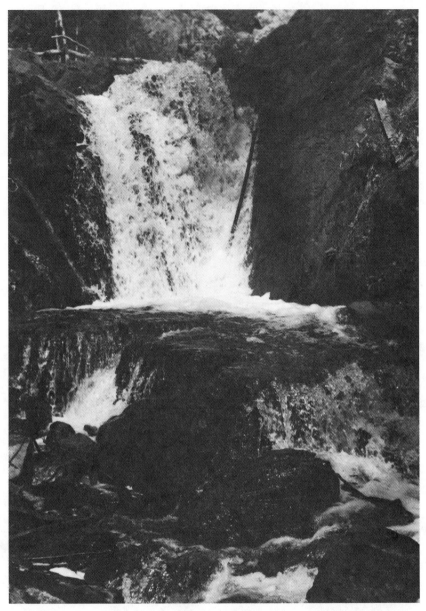

Schweitzer Falls

trail road on the right. (You have gone too far if you reach Co. Rd. ML on the left. Turn around and return to the first trail road to the left.) Schweitzer Falls is about a quarter of a mile down this dirt road. This road is generally in very good condition and easily driveable. But because of a large rock that was sticking up during our visit, we chose to park on the main road and walk the quarter mile to the falls.

As an alternate route to the falls, stay on Co. Rd. 565 until it crosses Schweitzer Creek, just past the junction with Co. Rd. ML. Park in the bridge area and walk upstream about a quarter of a mile.

WARNER FALLS

Warner Creek, Palmer

You can view Warner Falls from the side of the highway, but you should also take a short trail to its beginning. There, grassy, flat banks guide the small, clear stream down a few drops and through a channel worn into the iron-colored rock. In a feathery rush of white water the stream drops about 20 feet over the rock shelf, then collects in a shallow pool at the base of the falls before meandering through the underbrush.

The best view of the falls themselves comes from the road about 400 feet downstream from where the trail begins.

The easy accessibility of this falls, while appealing, also has its drawbacks. Downstream from the falls the riverbed is littered with refuse, a tiring reminder of its proximity to "civilization."

Directions: From the IGA store on M-35 in the village of Palmer, go south on M-35 about a half mile to the falls, on the right. (Map, p. 32)

Warner Falls

ELY FALLS

Ely Creek, 4 miles southwest of Ishpeming

Though there isn't a formal, well-marked trail to Ely Falls, it isn't too hard to find and is worth the effort.

The route through the woods ends on a huge section of pink-tinged stone with a spectacular view across a valley. Colored cliffs on the oppposite side of the large ravine stand out from the greens of the forest, and the crest of the surrounding hills is crowned with a stand of pine, which rises straight from the rock. Below, Ely Creek runs through the center of the ravine but is hidden from view by a thick stand of trees. To get to the river and falls you must scramble down about 35 feet to the base of the rounded wall of rock. A slippery layer of moss partly covers the rock, so watch your footing.

The falls itself is small, dropping a total of about 10 feet in several stages as the creek runs through a thicket of trees and bushes. When we visited, we were disappointed to find that the water both smelled and looked contaminated. Our cousin, who had visited the falls only a week before, reported that the water was crystal-clear then. So hopefully, the pollution was an unusual and isolated happening.

Directions: From downtown Ishpeming go west on Business Route M-28 past Robbins Flooring Mill, on the left, then another .2 miles to Washington Street. Turn left (south) onto Washington Street and go one mile to Co. Rd. 581. Turn right (west) onto Co. Rd. 581, also called Saginaw Street, and go approximately two miles to a fork in the road. Take the left fork (Co. Rd. 581) and go another 1.4 miles to a blacktop road, on the left

just before a brick church. Turn left (east) onto this road and go approximately 2.2 miles to a stop sign at a "T" intersection.

The quarter-mile route through the woods to the falls begins on the east side of that intersection. We turned right (south) at the stop sign, parked about 200 feet down the road, then crossed the road and found one of several faint trails which lead up, over and down a hill to the falls. As many trails criss-cross the area, we recommend that you mark your path on your way to the falls. (We hang red ribbons on trees, then remove them on the way out.)   (Photo p. 36)

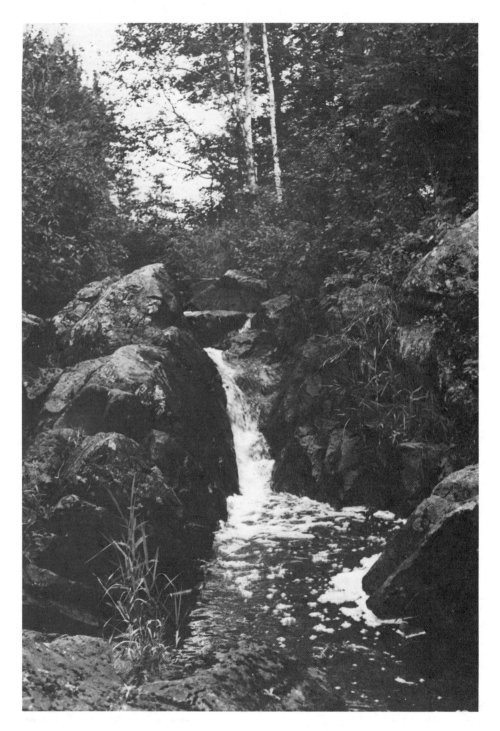

Ely Falls (p. 35)

WHITE CITY FALLS

Middle Branch Escanaba River, 7 miles southwest of Ishpeming

White City Falls, with a total drop of about 12 feet, is not large, but its design is unique and interesting. And it's only a few minutes' walk to the crest of a huge rounded section of stone, from which you view the falls, at the water's edge.

The river here narrows as it passes over a large rock bluff creased with cracks and fissures. One side of this bluff has dropped several inches lower than the other, and the river rushes down this natural line to the head of the falls, where the edge of the rock cuts back into the bluff at a sharp angle. The water then drops down in a sheet, half hidden from sight, between the two sections of stone into a large pool at the base of the falls.

Directions: From downtown Ishpeming go west on Business Route M-28 past Robbins Flooring Mill, on the left, then another .2 miles to Washington Street.

Turn left (south) onto Washington Street and go one mile to Co. Rd. 581. Turn right (west) onto Co. Rd. 581, also called Saginaw Street, and go approximately 5.5 miles to Co. Rd. CG. Turn left (south) onto Co. Rd. CG and go a little less than a mile to a fork. Take the left fork and go approximately 1.2 miles to another fork. This time take the right fork (which is obviously more used and in better condition) and go about .2 miles to where the road turns into a trail road. If you are driving a car, you should park in this area and continue on foot. We, however, continued in a truck another .4 miles to a trail on the right, which deadends at a parking spot. We parked our truck there and—after visiting the falls, which are only 150 feet away—had enough room to back onto the main trail and turn around.

(Map, p. 38)

BLACK RIVER FALLS

Black River, 8 miles southwest of Ishpeming

The short, easy trail to Black River Falls winds through such a beautiful stretch of pine forest that the walk would be well worth taking just for itself. This area was once a state-forest campground, and the remains of long-deserted roads angle off through the stately pines, which stretch far overhead. Though the towering pines command your attention as you walk to the falls, the area is not thickly wooded, and sunlight brightens the entire forest floor. At its beginning the trail is smooth and flat, then imbedded logs create steps as it drops slightly to cross over the face of a rock bluff and over the edge to the falls.

There, a foaming mass of copper-tinted water cuts between two huge rock bluffs, then tumbles over black rocks hidden in midstream. A small rock outcropping tries to break through in the center of the strong flow, but the water slides over it in waves, covering it with a thin layer of clear water. At the base and in front of this 20-foot-high falls, a large island divides the river into two unequally sized streams. You can cross on a small footbridge to the island for a clear head-on view of the waterfall. As the river widens out on the other downstream side of the island, it forms a small pool whose surface is littered with stray bubbles from the pounding of the falls upstream.

The power of this falls is delicately balanced by its placement in a still and silent landscape. The banks of the river are hedged by dense woods, which thin out dramatically near the huge escarpment of rock that borders the falls. Pale grasses and small ferns peek out from fissures in the side of the rock, whose summit is crowned only with red pine. A light dusting of green moss adds color to the rock and a softness to the falls.

Directions: From downtown Ishpeming go west on Business Route M-28 past Robbins Flooring Mill, on the left, then another .2 miles to Washington Street. Turn left (south) onto Washington Street and go one mile to Co. Rd. 581. Turn right (west) onto Co. Rd. 581, also called Saginaw Street, and go approximately 7.5 miles, across the Escanaba River, to the Black River Pathway on the right. Turn right (west) onto Black River Pathway and go about .6 miles to a fork. Take the right fork and go about .2 miles to a trail road on the right. Turn right, onto this trail road, and go .4 miles to a parking area marked by a line of large stones. The trail to the falls begins on the right hand side of these stones as you face them.

34

CAPS CREEK FALLS

Caps Creek, 5 miles south of Republic

The falls is on private property.

35

TROUT FALLS

Trout Falls Creek, 3 miles south of Republic

Directions: We did not visit this falls as there was no trail to it and no room to park on the side of the road near it. However, if you would like to try, here's how to get there: On M-95 from Republic, go south approximately 1.2 miles to a set of railroad tracks. Cross the tracks, then turn right (west) onto Co. Rd. 601, the first road after the tracks. Go approximately 1.7 miles to Trout Falls Creek. The falls are located about a quarter of a mile upstream.

DEE LUNDEEN FALLS

West Branch Peshekee River, 5 miles northwest of Champion

We take particular pleasure in telling you about Dee Lundeen Falls because it has not been included on any county maps or list of waterfalls that we know of. We don't know why this falls has been overlooked. It is beautiful and shouldn't be missed.

With stately pines standing guard in the heart of Marquette County's moose country, the fast-flowing Peshekee River rushes toward a rocky bluff. The water then skates over the slightly angled surface of smooth red stone, turns abruptly

right, then heads straight down the iron-colored rocks in a 10-foot drop. Huge boulders are scattered in such a pattern to the bottom of the hill that the water rushes around and over them in three distinct sections.

The river is about 30 feet wide at the base of the falls, and its strength couples with the looming bluff and iron-colored rocks to create an image of wild grandeur that lingers in your mind.

Pilings left over from an old rock-and-log dam jut from the water behind the

Dee Lundeen Falls

falls, and hundreds of iron pins, which held the logs together, are scattered over the ground.

Directions: On US-41/M-28, go west from Champion approximately 2.5 miles to the Peshekee River, then continue another three miles to a trail on the right (just past Herb and Mary's bar, then a Methodist Church, both on the left), near signs which point to the Methodist Institute. Unless you have a truck or four-wheel-drive vehicle, we recommend parking there and walking the 2.5 miles to the falls.

We drove in on the trail for about a mile in our two-wheel-drive truck, but then had to stop at a bad spot in the road and continue on foot. A four-wheel-drive vehicle, however, could easily negotiate the next 1 1/4 miles to an old wooden bridge.

The walking trail begins at this neglected bridge, which is now suitable only for foot traffic, and even then use caution when crossing. The trail to the falls is an easy two-track road, but the terrain is rough and the hills can be tiring. Follow the two-track about a quarter of a mile as it turns sharply right, then ends abruptly in a small clearing. A five-minute walk through the thick, low-lying area directly across the clearing ends at the river and, a few yards upstream, the falls.

Because this is an active logging area and many trails converge here, we

strongly recommend getting current directions either from the DNR office in Ishpeming or the Mead Paper Co., Peshekee Yard, on the south side of US-41 shortly after you cross the Peshekee River. Though we had no directions to the falls, we knew its location by checking old topographical maps. By staying on the most-used trail and using our compass at every turn, we made it to the falls with no problem.

37

CARP RIVER FALLS

Carp River, 8 1/2 miles west of Marquette

The trail to this falls begins upstream from Old US-41 west of Marquette but is

posted, "Private Property."

38
MORGAN FALLS

39
UNNAMED FALLS

40
CARP RIVER FALLS

Carp River, 2 1/2 miles southwest of Marquette

There are four very accessible falls in the Morgan Creek area, all located near the side of the road. Three can easily be reached from one parking area.

The first, Morgan Falls, is more of a rapids than a falls. As Morgan Creek passes beneath a steel bridge (near where you have parked), it begins to descend and, in a 100-foot-long section of rapids and small falls, twists and runs swiftly past the thick forest which grows atop the steep banks.

Unnamed Falls, Carp River

To get to the unnamed falls and Carp River Falls, from the steel bridge walk back along the entrance road about 400 yards (you will hear a waterfalls on the right). A short walk from the road down a steep bank leads right to the top of the most impressive falls in the area.

Framed by the blackness of wet rock and the emerald greens of the forest, this unnamed falls is a beautiful sight. It is wide, stretching about 15 feet across the rough stone cliff, and it is loud. The main section drops nearly 20 feet in a brilliant, roaring curtain of white. Dappled sections of sunlight reach between the thick layer of leaves overhead to highlight portions of the rushing water.

To get to Carp River Falls, cross Morgan Creek above the unnamed falls and walk about 100 feet downstream to where Morgan Creek joins the Carp River. Follow the Carp River upstream a little less than half a mile. There is no trail, but by following the riverbanks you can easily reach the falls, which drops over the rock bed a total of about 10 feet in two stages. There are two Carp River Falls in Marquette County—one west of Marquette, which is on private property, and this small falls, which is open to the public.

(Continued on p. 43)

UNNAMED FALLS

Morgan Creek, 3 1/2 miles southwest of Marquette

Deep in the shadows of the forest southwest of Marquette, Morgan Creek cuts through a ravine as it meanders to a peaceful, relaxing falls. The water makes several drops—six feet at the highest—in lazy streams over and around square sections of rock which resemble an ancient wall. Moss, which covers the flat surfaces of these rocks, provides a soft cushion for the surrounding water as it slips by. Ferns and other delicate plants, which layer the low banks, line the creek with a border of green. This entire area, for perhaps 100 feet, repeats the beautiful pattern of water falling slowly over levels of dark rock.

Directions: From US-41/M-28 west of Marquette, turn south onto Co. Rd. 492 (just west of a Pizza Hut at the west side of Marquette Mall). (If you are coming from the east you cannot turn left from US-41/M-28. Go one block farther, make a U turn, return one block and turn right, onto Co. Rd. 492.) After about two blocks the road forks. Continue on Co. Rd. 492, the right fork, approximately four miles to Morgan Meadow Drive.

Turn left (south) onto Morgan Meadow Drive, cross Morgan Creek, then turn left (east) onto the first trail road. Go a short distance on this trail road across a wooden bridge and continue approximately another half mile to where the creek again crosses under the road. Just past that point is a small parking area on the right. The trail to the falls begins across the road and follows a ravine that begins where the road crosses the stream.

Note: When you look at a Marquette County map, it appears as though you can continue east on this trail road to Morgan Falls (#38), Carp River Falls (# 40) and an unnamed falls (#39). We do not recommend attempting a straight-through trip in anything other than a four-wheel drive vehicle. And even that will not necessarily guarantee that you'll complete the crossing. The trail road is actually an abandoned railroad bed, and two bridges have replaced trestles. It is at those two bridges that the road is at its worst.

We drove a four-wheel drive truck on our most recent trip to this area, but we still decided to walk. We have walked the entire distance between the two bridges, and there are no waterfalls in that area. Therefore we recommend that you play it safe by following the directions printed in the description of the three aforementioned falls and drive in a short distance on a good trail road. (Map, p. 44)

CARP RIVER FALLS
(Continued from p. 42)

Directions: From where US-41/M-28 makes a 90-degree turn in Marquette, go about a half mile south on US-41/M-28 to a signal light at Genesee Street. Turn right (west) onto Genesee Street and go one block to Division Street. Turn left (south) onto Division Street (which becomes Co. Rd. 553 as you leave Marquette) and go approximately 1.7 miles to a trail road on the right, just before reaching the Marquette Mountain Ski Resort. Turn right (west) onto the trail road and go approximately 1.4 miles to an old steel bridge. Park before crossing the bridge (the road on the other side is not in very good condition). (Map, p.44)

DEAD RIVER FALLS

Dead River, 3 miles northwest of Marquette

The Dead River runs through a huge gorge, and from its top you view the falls. The falls, which drops only a few feet, is mostly hidden, however, by bushes growing in front and to the sides. The entire area, in fact, is covered with bushes and small trees, which effectively screen most of the river. Huge strands of weeds and algae, which ripple in the river's murky green current, indicate that the water is probably being warmed farther upstream. If it is, the source of the heat is a mystery.

Directions: From US-41/M-28 west of Marquette, turn right (north) onto Wright Street (the first street west of a K mart store) and gradually bear right (east) about a half mile to Forestville Road. Turn left (north) onto Forestville Road and go about 2.5 miles, remaining on the paved road as it curves sharply left and reaches a power plant at its end.

The trail to Dead River Falls follows electrical wires up a hill and through the forest behind the powerhouse. About 100 yards past the end of the main hill, a section of an aqueduct is exposed, and on it someone has painted "falls" and an arrow to the left. Follow that trail to the river.

REANY FALLS

Reany Creek, 3 miles northwest of Marquette

As Reany Creek completes its journey to the Dead River, it creates a band of white as it rushes over the rocks in an extensive series of drops. The rock which lines the stream is an interesting mix of rich browns and dark grays, and the greens of the forest shade the entire area. You can see portions of this beautiful little falls from your car. But the falls extends upstream perhaps 200 feet, and you really should explore the trails that run up both sides of the stream.

Directions: From US-41/M-28 west of Marquette, turn right (north) onto Wright Street (the first street west of a K mart store) and gradually bear right (east) about a half mile to Forestville Road. Turn left (north) onto Forestville Road and go about 2.5 miles, remaining on the paved road as it curves sharply left and reaches a power plant at its end.

Just as you pass a bridge before entering the power house area, you will see the bottom part of the falls to the right. There is no parking space at the bridge, so park your vehicle in the power house area and walk back about 200 yards on Forestville Road to the falls.

LITTLE GARLIC FALLS

Little Garlic River, 11 miles north of Marquette

Directions: From Wright Street on the north edge of Northern Michigan University in Marquette, turn north onto Sugar Loaf Avenue, which turns into Co. Rd. 550, and go approximately 11.5 miles to the Little Garlic River. Cross this popular trout stream, then turn into a parking area on the left. The falls are about a 2.5-mile walk upstream.

If you have a four-wheel-drive vehicle, you can go on Co. Rd. 550 another quarter of a mile north of the parking area to a trail road on the left. Turn left, follow the trail road about a mile and a half to the river, then walk upstream about a mile to the falls.

45

BUSHY CREEK FALLS

(Also known as Yellow Dog Falls and Yellow Dog Slate Falls)

Yellow Dog River, 7 miles southeast of Big Bay

The trail to Bushy Creek Falls rises steeply through the Huron Mountains to a huge outcropping of rock on the banks of the Yellow Dog River. Directly in front of this outcropping, the falls gradually drops about 20 feet through a deep, 10-foot-wide chasm cut by the river through the stone, then continues downstream in a large section of rapids. The centuries-long pounding of the falls has formed a wide, deep pool at their base, and the surrounding stone shines a wet, glossy black. The banks gradually pull back from the falls and rise to become part of

the huge rock outcropping upon which you stand. The bright, almost-white moss which covers this rock mass provides a complementary foreground to the vista's contrast of colors.

Directions: There are two routes to this falls. The first (the one we used) is relatively more complicated, but involves a shorter walk. The second is easier to follow but entails a much harder walk.

Route 1: From Wright Street on the north edge of Northern Michigan University in Marquette, turn north onto Sugar Loaf Avenue, which turns into Co. Rd.

550, and go approximately 22 miles to Co. Rd. 510 (about 2.5 miles before Big Bay). Turn left (south) onto Co. Rd. 510 and go about five miles (bearing sharply left past Triple A Road at about three miles) to Bushy Creek Truck Trail, on the left directly across from a yellow steel post.

Turn left (east) onto this good two-track and go about 1.4 miles to another trail road, on the right. Continue straight (the road is very bad ahead, so we recommend parking near the fork and proceeding on foot) a short distance to a washed-out area where the trail bears left. Go another quarter of a mile to a large clearing of loose sand. It is a short

walk down a steep hill on the right, then slighty upstream, to the falls. On a quiet day you can hear the falls from the top of the hill.

Route 2: From Wright Street on the north edge of Northern Michigan University in Marquette, turn north onto Sugar Loaf Avenue, which turns into Co. Rd. 550, and go approximately 22 miles to Co. Rd. 510 (about 2.5 miles before Big Bay). Turn left (south) onto Co. Rd. 510 and go approximately 6.3 miles to the Yellow Dog River. Cross the river and park on the left. Follow the trail downstream, on the right bank, for about 1.5 miles to the falls.   (Map, p. 49)

Bushy Creek Falls

ALDER FALLS

Alder Creek, 2 1/2 miles southeast of Big Bay

In a series of short drops, Alder Creek falls about six feet then plunges 30 feet over the side of a sharply rising rock bluff to create the main section of Alder Falls. The rock bluff seems to come out of nowhere, but looking back through the trees you can see its unusual outline dividing the forest on either side of the falls. The falls covers a 15-foot-wide section of the stoney ridge with a blanket of moving whiteness, which contrasts sharply with the dusty greens of the surrounding forest. Above the falls, a few fallen logs have created a natural bridge and a frame, beneath which the water rushes in a frothing mass. At the base of the falls the water bubbles around several large boulders which have fallen to create a necklace of stepping stones.

Directions: From Wright Street on the north edge of Northern Michigan University in Marquette, turn north onto Sugar Loaf Avenue, which turns into Co. Rd. 550. After driving approximately 21 miles (about 3.5 miles before Big Bay) look for a paved road to Alder, on the right. Continue on Co. Rd. 550 just beyond the road to Alder, then turn left (south) onto a trail road. This trail road immediately forks; take the left fork approximately .3 miles to a washed-out area. You may want to park your vehicle in a turnout there, but we continued in a two-wheel-drive truck with no problem.

Whether walking or driving, continue down the trail road for approximately .4 miles to the trail to the falls on the right. (If you come to some cottages on the left, you have gone too far.) It's only about a quarter of a mile to the falls, but the trail descends steeply down the side of a hill. The smooth ground is covered with rust-colored pine needles, and the surrounding forest is so thick with pines and hardwoods that only a few smaller trees have managed to poke their way through the branches overhead.

Alder Falls

Marquette County

Big Bay

Lake Independence

Co. Rd. 550

Alder

Co. Rd. 510

ALDER FALLS

Triple A Rd.

Co. Rd. 510

Co. Rd. 550

N

Miles

0   1/2   1

Yellow steel post

BUSHY CREEK FALLS

Yellow Dog River

Marquette County

Ely Falls (p. 35

Dee Lundeen Falls (p. 40)

Marquette County

WYLIE FALLS
(Also known as Wylie Falls Dam)

Yellow Dog River, 9 miles southwest of Big Bay

Access along the main trail to this falls, located about three miles upstream from Pinnacle Falls (#48), ends at a cable strung by owners as a request not to cross their private property.

We searched for about three hours and finally found a way around the private property. However, that route involves a mile hike on an overgrown trail through a remote area. Therefore, we do not recommend visiting Wylie Falls.

48

PINNACLE FALLS
(Also known as Pinnacle Falls Dam)

Yellow Dog River, 8 miles southwest of Big Bay

By following directions obtained from a local tourist information group, we walked a wide, clear trail to this falls, which is sandwiched between two towering hills in one of the most rugged sections of the Huron Mountains.

We later found out, however, that the falls and trail to it are on private property.

49

TWIN FALLS
(Also known as Hogback Falls)

East Branch Salmon Trout River, 5 1/2 miles west of Big Bay

Though this falls is located on a public access road about six miles west of Big Bay, we do not recommend travel to it.

The main trail road is generally impassable, plus many other trails converge in this remote area.

Marquette County

50

CLIFF FALLS
(Also known as 40-Foot Falls)

Cliff River, 12 miles west of Big Bay

Couched in the seclusion of the Huron Mountains, Cliff Falls is a place of serenity. Tall hardwoods stretch silently overhead to frame the vibrant energy of the river's strong current and the white foaming falls.

The 15-foot-wide river approaches along the face of a steep rock outcropping, then drops at least 40 feet in several stages and in separate streams divided by sections of moss-covered rock. The angle of the falls is steep but not sheer, and toward the bottom it begins to flatten out until it gently meets a pool at its base. A light dusting of bright green moss covers

the rough surface of a dry rocky area to the left of the falls. This section is swallowed up by the river in high water, when the falls doubles in size.

Directions: There are two routes to this falls, one from the Big Bay area of Marquette County and the other from Baraga County. We strongly recommend driving to the falls from Baraga County because the route from Big Bay not only takes you through some of the most remote areas of Marquette County, but is also complicated by its intersection with many unmarked trails.

From Baraga County: From US-41 in L'Anse, take Broad Street to Skanee Road (Main Street), then go east out of L'anse on Skanee Road approximately 18.5 miles to a fork in the road. Take Eric Road, the right fork, (the left fork is Portice Road) past Big Eric's Bridge State Forest Campground (at 1.1 miles), then continue straight ahead across the bridge and follow the main road (Big Bay Road) about 6.7 miles to a trail road on the left. (If you pass some junked cars in a clearing on your right, you have gone too far. Turn around and turn right, onto the first trail road you reach.)

Turn onto this trail road (you are on the correct road if, after a very short distance, you see another trail road heading left back to the main road) and go .5 miles past a small building on the right; another .4 miles past a cabin on the right with a sign reading, "Cliff Falls Hunting Club;" then another .3 miles to a beaver pond on the left. Just past the beaver pond, the road forks. Take the right fork approximately .9 miles to the top of a hill

Cliff Falls

and a foot trail on the right. Follow that trail down a hill about 75 feet to the river at the top of the falls.

From Marquette County: From Wright Street on the north edge of Northern Michigan University in Marquette, turn north onto Sugar Loaf Avenue, which turns into Co. Rd. 550, and go approximately 22 miles to Co. Rd. 510 (about 2.5 miles before Big Bay). Turn left (south) onto Co. Rd. 510 and go approximately three miles to Triple A Road, shortly after Co. Rd 510 bears sharply left. Turn right (west) onto Triple A Road and follow it about 13.3 miles to Ford Road, marked by a large clear-cut area just before Triple A Road turns sharply left (south). Turn right (north) onto Ford

Road (a fairly wide, sandy two-track) and go about 4.5 miles (just past a clearing on the left with some junked cars) to the trail road to Cliff Falls, on the right.

Turn onto this trail road (you are on the correct road if, after a very short distance, you see another trail road heading left back to the main road) and go .5 miles past a small building on the right; another .4 miles past a cabin on the right with a sign reading, "Cliff Falls Hunting Club;" then another .3 miles to a beaver pond on the left. Just past the beaver pond, the road forks. Take the right fork approximately .9 miles to the top of a hill and a foot trail on the right. Follow that trail down a hill about 75 feet to the river at the top of the falls.

51

80-FOOT FALLS
(Also known as Ives Falls)

River Styx at Ives Lake Outlet

52

MIDDLE FALLS

Salmon Trout River

53

UPPER FALLS

West Branch, Salmon Trout River

54

LOWER FALLS

Snake Creek

55

MOUNTAIN STREAM FALLS

Mountain Stream

These falls—located within the boundaries of the Huron Mountain Club, west of Big Bay—are closed to the public.

MARQUETTE COUNTY DAM SITES

1-D
CATARACT ESCANABA FALLS
Escanaba River, 3 miles north of Princeton

The road to this dam is gated and
marked with a "No Trespassing" sign.
According to local residents, there is no
falls, only a dam, at this site.

The following Marquette County falls,
which are included on some old lists, are
not marked on maps, and we could not
find anyone who had ever heard of them.
If you have information regarding these
falls, please contact the authors.

Little Boney Falls—Escanaba River, south of Gwinn

Jewell Falls—Escanaba River, north of Gwinn

Big Garlic Falls—Garlic River, northwest of Marquette

Cliff Peshekee Falls—Cliff Peshekee River, west of Big Bay
We found no Cliff Peshekee River in
this area. By studying maps of the area,
we believe this is the same as Cliff Falls,
also known as 40-Foot Falls (#50) on the
Cliff River.

BARAGA COUNTY

Lower West Branch Falls (p. 60)

An interesting mixture of both natural and historical attractions await visitors to Baraga County, which borders the southeastern edge of Keweenaw Bay.

Pointe Abbaye—the tip of a finger of land which separates Huron Bay from Keweenaw Bay—itself is worth a day of peaceful wandering along its trails and Lake Superior beaches. The view from the point is beautiful and includes the elusive Huron Islands, to the east, and the Huron Mountains, to the southeast.

One of Baraga County's mountains, 1,978.82-foot Mt. Arvon, is Michigan's highest point. (For decades, nearby Mt. Curwood claimed the title as the state's highest "peak," but according to official 1985 Geologic Survey measurements, Mt. Arvon is higher by a whopping 11 inches.) At that modest elevation, Mt. Arvon is snow-capped only when winter white blankets the entire county. Snowstorms here can be fierce, but because of the moderating influence of Lake Superior, overall winter temperatures average around 20 degrees, mild compared to the rest of the peninsula.

The land, here, however is rugged and wild, with thick forests spreading south from Lake Superior. An impressive 80% of Baraga County's acreage is open to hunting, and game and wildlife is abundant. If you're lucky, you may even catch a glimpse of a moose. Transplanted Canadian moose were released near Michigamme in 1985 and again in 1987 and since then have spread throughout the Huron Mountain area of Baraga and Marquette counties. (One has even been spotted as far east as Luce County.)

Baraga County is also home to the Keweenaw Bay Indian Community, and the area is rich in Indian lore and history. (For an enlightening experience in native American culture, attend the Indian Spiritual Dance, held at Baraga annually on the fourth weekend in July.) Archeological excavations at Sand Point, for example, have unearthed the remains of communities dating from the 12th century. And five miles from L'Anse at the Pinery, the public is welcome to walk through rows of gravesites at an Indian burial ground which dates from the 1840s. Picket fences surround some of the plots, and small wooden houses—their surface weathered by constant exposure to the elements—cover many of the oldest. It's somehow silently reassuring to see the remnants of this burial tradition, which gradually disappeared due to the influence of Christian missionaires.

The influence of missionaries, among the first white visitors to the area, is still felt in other ways, also. Baraga County, in fact, is named after Bishop Baraga, a Jesuit priest who began the area's first mission at Assinins in 1843. High atop Red Rocks Bluff, between Baraga and L'Anse, stands a unique and beautiful monument to that clergyman and his work. Called the Shrine of the Snowshoe Priest, a 35-foot-high burnished-gold figure of Bishop Baraga—a seven-foot-high cross in his outstretched hand and 26-foot snowshoes leaning against his side—towers over the wide expanse of Keweenaw Bay. The statue balances on a cloud of stainless steel from which wooden arches swoop down to five teepees, symbols of the five major missions Baraga founded.

Another Jesuit, Father Rene Mennard, came to the area in 1660 and later constructed the Northwest's first church at Pequaming, seven miles north of L'anse. Two and a half centuries later, Henry Ford picked Pequaming as the site for his upper-peninsula lumber and iron-mining interests as well as his summer home. Today, Pequaming is only a haven for ghost-town fanciers.

For more specific information about Baraga County and its attractions you may contact the following:

Baraga County Chamber of Commerce
P.O. Box 556
Baraga MI 49908

Department of Natural Resources
District 1 Office
North US-41, Box 440
Baraga MI 49908

Baraga County Historical Society
County Court House
L'Anse MI 49946

Upper Peninsula Travel and Recreation
   Association
P.O. Box 400
Iron Mountain MI 49801

BIG ERIC'S FALLS
(Also known as Lower Huron Falls)

Huron River, 6 miles southeast of Skanee

Just below Big Eric's Bridge the Huron River drops in three sections to form Big Eric's Falls (sometimes known as Lower Huron Falls). At the first, the river divides into five streams across its entire width, then drops abruptly about four feet over a small ridge. Several yards farther downstream the river contracts and falls again, this time dropping about five feet over the smooth stone.

The rocky banks here fall back from the river several feet to form a large open area around the water, and as the stone dries, this border turns a golden tan. Rocks scattered throughout the water downstream form a small rapids between the second and third falls.

The third and smallest falls divides into three equal sections as it pounds about three feet over a rocky ledge. The churning waters below leave a triangle of white, foamy water which gradually trails away downstream. At the side of this falls stands a lone tall pine, its wide branches shading the bubbling water below. Downstream, the river divides around a small green island covered with trees and bushes that effectively screen the rest of the river from view.

The river here is a popular spot with both fall salmon fishermen and spring steelheaders. When the steelhead run is in full swing, the banks are lined with eager fishermen trying their luck in one of the many pools in this section of the river. Trails head downstream from the bridge along both banks. On the west side of the river is a state-forest campground.

Directions: From L'Anse go northeast on Skanee Road (called Main Street in the city of L'Anse) approximately 18.5 miles to a fork. The left fork is Portice Road and the right fork is Eric's Road. Take Eric's Road approximately 1.2 miles to Big Eric's Bridge Campground. The falls begins at the bridge and runs downstream. (Across Eric's Bridge, the road becomes Big Bay Road, which leads about 6.7 miles to the trail to Cliff Falls, #50, in Marquette County.)

WEST BRANCH FALLS

West Branch Huron River, 6 1/2 miles southeast of Skanee

Three distinctly beautiful drops make up West Branch Falls. And as an added adventure, you must ford a river to reach them.

At the first drop, farthest upstream, the 12-foot-wide river narrows to two feet as it rushes through a narrow chute it has carved deep into the rock. To the left of this chute, slate banks angle steeply up to a carpet of thick, deep-green moss. Pines, which cling tenaciously to the rocks high up the side of the steep banks, send their thick, dusty-green branches bending over the falls. Downstream, boughs continue to reach over the river from the forest of stately pines and scattered birch.

Just before the second section of falls is one of the best pools we've found for swimming or wading. The river there widens to about 15 feet, and the small rocks and pebbles on the bottom of the pool are distinctly visible through the crystal-clear water. The surrounding banks are not only quite steep, but also—because of countless chipped-out sections—rough. Moss lightly covers some of the stone, causing it to blend into the shadows of the pines above. At the bottom of this long pool the river drops, but only about two feet, and the bushy green fronds of thick ferns, which begin to line the banks, brush the cool water.

The river then turns to the left, and heads about 100 yards to the largest falls. There, the river flows over a section of steeply angled stone in a slide of water which drops about 30 feet over the smooth rock. Toward the bottom, the falls

splits into three streaks of white against black. A steep bank of rough stone, moss-covered near the top, borders the falls on the left. On the right, huge gray boulders—which seem to have spilled over the side of the falls to line the banks downstream—guides the flow. Also to the right, a small stream that had been separated from the main falls emerges from behind a rock to join with the river once again.

Directions: From L'Anse go northeast on Skanee Road (called Main Street in the city of L'Anse) approximately 18.2 miles to Black Creek Road (also known as West Branch Huron River Road) on the right. (If you reach the fork at Portice Road ad Eric's Road, you have gone about a quarter of a mile too far.) Turn right (south) onto Black Creek Road and go approximately 1.6 miles to a trail on the left. Turn left (east) onto this trail and go approximately .2 miles to the west branch of the Huron River.

To visit this falls you must ford a river, so we urge extreme caution. Do not attempt to cross during high-water periods or during threatening weather.

Cross the river and take the road up the hill on the right. Go approximately .6 miles and park your vehicle on the edge of the trail in one of the few spots wide enough to turn around. It is just a short walk west to the river, but mark a trail for yourself to guide you back out. At the river you may have to walk a short way up or downstream guided by the sound of the falls. (Map, p. 59)

Big Falls (p. 62)

West Branch Falls, Lower Section

BIG FALLS

East Branch Huron River, 7 miles southeast of Skanee

While trying to find this falls, we had to ford the west branch of the Huron River with our truck, which made us even more determined to reach it. The reward was worth the effort.

Surrounded by thick hardwood forest, the east branch of the Huron River flows along the bottom of a gorge it has cut and shaped in its centuries-long rush through the thin layers of stone. In this gorge, the river divides, then drops 20 feet in two sections. The falls on the right forms a near-curtain of white as it drops suddenly from a rough stone ledge. The drop on the left, on the other hand, is gradual. The river there runs over a beautiful section of terraced rock, each step in line with the others to form a perfectly balanced image of layered water. At the base of the falls, the river converges in a large pool, and between the two falls, sections of a brown rock, topped by thick green bushes, turn light tan as they dry.

Downstream, steep, rough walls of layered stone, which has been chiseled out in bits and pieces by the strength of the river, continue to guide the water.

Directions: From L'Anse go northeast on Skanee Road (called Main Street in the city of L'Anse) approximately 18.2 miles to Black Creek Road (also known as West Branch Huron River Road) on the right. (If you reach the fork at Portice Road and Eric's Road, you have gone about a quarter of a mile too far.) Turn right (south) onto Black Creek Road and go approximately 1.6 miles to a trail on the left. Turn left (east) onto this trail and go approximately .2 miles to the west branch of the Huron River.

To visit this falls you must ford a river, so we urge extreme caution. Do not attempt to cross during high-water periods or during threatening weather.

Cross the river and take the trail road to the left, approximately two miles to the east branch of the Huron River. The road turns to the right just as it reaches the river, and the falls are down the steep bank on the left.

(Map, p. 59) (Photo, p. 61)

EAST BRANCH FALLS

East Branch Huron River, 6 1/2 miles southeast of Skanee

Even though it is located in the vicinity of Big Falls, because of often-impassable trail conditions and the remoteness of the area, we do not recommend travel to this falls.

ERIC'S FALLS
(Also known as Lower Letherby Falls)

West Branch Huron River, 8 miles southeast of Skanee

About 100 feet from Black Creek Road, the shallow west branch of the Huron River drops about six feet over a stone ridge that extends from the water through the surrounding forest. The river divides into delicate streams of white, which course over the smooth dark stone, then rejoin as they reach for the bottom. The stones that make up the ridge under the falls have developed very interesting shapes. Smoothed out with curving surfaces and rounded sides, they appear to take on some of the liquid properties of the water that courses over them. A fallen log—its base resting near a small pool at the base—spans the falls from top to bottom. Many of the living trees that surround the falls extend precariously over the water's surface. Their branches diffuse the bright sunlight and bathe the falls in quiet shade.

As the river continues downstream, it drops over several layers of flat steps every few feet. The stream remains shallow, and bushy growth pushes out from the forest over the pebbles and small stones that line the low banks.

Directions: From L'Anse go northeast on Skanee Road (called Main Street in the city of L'Anse) approximately 18.2 miles to Black Creek Road (also called West Branch Huron River Road) on the right. (If you reach the fork of Portice and Eric's roads, you have gone about a quarter of a mile too far.) Turn right (south) onto Black Creek Road and go approximately 4.8 miles to the west branch of the Huron River. The falls are a short distance downstream. (Map, p. 59)

61

LETHERBY FALLS

West Branch Huron River, 9 miles southeast of Skanee

62

UPPER LETHERBY FALLS

West Branch Huron River, 9 1/2 miles southeast of Skanee

Both falls, located south of Eric's (Lower Letherby) Falls, are on private property, and access to them is blocked by closed gates in the area. Therefore, we do not recommend travel to these two waterfalls.

63

SLATE RIVER FALLS

Slate River, 3 1/2 miles southwest of Skanee

White water billows over a ledge of sharply angled rock as the Slate River drops 25 feet. From the base of the falls, a huge, calm pool extends downstream past banks peppered with with small light-colored stones. To the left of the main flow, small white strands of water trace their way over this rough stone. On

both sides of the falls, the rock has been pushed up to leave a flat surface covered with emerald-green moss. On the left, these rocks rise in several layers, like bright-green steps, to a crest, where pines extend back into the forest.

Directions: As you approach L'Anse on US-41 from the south, turn right, onto Broad Street, and go approximately .6 miles to the blinker light on Main Street in downtown L'Anse. Turn right (east) onto Main Street and go about 11 miles (Main Street turns into Skanee Road as you leave L'Anse) to the Slate River. Cross the river (just past Arvon Road), turn south onto the first trail on the right, and park. (The Slate River and the Slate River Falls Trail are marked with a sign on Skanee Road). The half-mile trail to Slate Falls follows the banks of the river.

BLACK SLATE FALLS

QUARTZITE FALLS

Slate River, 6 miles southwest of Skanee

Only a few hundred yards of the Slate River separate Black Slate Falls and Quartzite Falls. The short, easy trail to them runs through forest not thick enough to stop the sun from breaking through the leaves overhead. Slabs of mossy rock are scattered throughout the woods, and occasional wild lilies add a brush of color.

Black Slate Falls begins as a rapids which runs for several yards before dropping four feet over the edge of a rock formation. This main section of falls spans the 20-foot wide river in three distinct sections, which trail in thin streams over the side of the rock. Mossy rock-lined banks—one softly sloping, the other a sheer wall—guide the water. Downstream, the river forms a chute, through which the water rushes over smooth rock on its few-hundred-feet journey to Quartzite Falls.

The rapids ignore a fallen log in the center as they make a gradual descent past three strips of grass-covered rock, then rush to the falls. There, the river curves slightly to the left as it drops over a slate ledge into a pool. The river drops a second, then a third time—about eight feet altogether. Each section is separated by a small pool, its smooth, dark surface hiding the depths below. Looking back from below the last of the falls, the scene is lovely. A brush of white, the first falls, tops the vista. A band of darkness is then connected through a series of trickling white streams to a second band of dark-

ness. The pattern repeats, until the river finally rushes past and is lost around a bend.

Each falls in this book is surrounded by its own unspoken, unseen history. Quartzite Falls is no different, except that here a bit of history remains in the form of a large hole back from the riverbanks at the top of the first falls. Littered now

(continued on p. 66)

BLACK SLATE/QUARTZITE FALLS
(Continued from p. 65)

with rust-colored leaves and pine needles, the excavation blends in with the surrounding forest, and few would notice it. Fewer still would wonder how it got there. The depression, in fact, was a test pit dug by prospectors as a prelude to the Arvon Slate Quarry, which opened in 1872. This quarry had a reputation for providing the best quality slate in the Midwest and was an integral part of the county's economy for many years. Now the hole serves only as a simple reminder of the changing needs of our society.

Directions: As you approach L'Anse on US-41 from the south, turn right, onto Broad Street, and go approximately .6 miles to the blinker light on Main Street in downtown L'Anse. Turn right (east) onto Main Street and go about 11 miles (Main Street turns into Skanee Road as you leave L'Anse) to Arvon Road, just before the Slate River. Turn right (south) onto Arvon Road and go approximately 3.3 miles to a trail on the left. (If you reach the point where Arvon Road bears sharply right, you have gone just a bit too far. The trail which continues straight from that point leads to the Arvon Slate Quarry Area.)

This trail to the river is very short, and though neither falls is marked with a sign, they are fairly easy to find. At the river, look for the remains of an old bridge. Black Slate Falls are a short distance upstream and Quartzite Falls a short distance downstream from that point.   *(Black Slate Falls photo, p. 84)*

Quartzite Falls

66

SILVER FALLS

(Also known as Lower Silver Falls)

67

UNNAMED FALLS

Silver River, 6 miles northeast of L'Anse

A short trail ends on a huge shelf of rock with a commanding view of Silver River and Silver Falls. The water below flows through rugged terrain. Huge boulders surround the river and thick, green forests close in on the flow as it repeatedly drops over even more boulders that litter its path.

A trail down to the base of the falls leads to a more intimate view. As you descend, the rock shelf you left behind gradually rises to top a steep wall of dark stone, which towers over the river, on the right. The left bank, though not as tall, is also steep and rugged, with huge sections of sharp rock pushing the forest back several feet.

The river here pulses through two chutes it has worn into the rock, and a long, thin island of stone remains to separate the two channels. Across the river, to the left, another area of stone, which runs through the pines, probably creates another falls and small island in the spring. At the base of the falls, the river forms a small sandy-bottomed pool—ideal for wading or fishing—then twists out of sight downstream.

As we were about to leave the area, we thought we heard another falls farther downstream. We were right. One hundred yards down the trail, the river froths for several yards down a three-foot-wide channel, then fans out into a six-foot drop of white water over the rough black rocks below. From there, hedged in by rocky

banks and dotted with huge boulders in midstream, the river rushes out of sight.

Directions: As you approach L'Anse on US-41 from the south, turn right, onto Broad Street, and go approximately .6 miles to the blinker light on Main Street in downtown L'Anse. Turn right (east) onto Main Street and go about 6.8 miles (Main Street turns into Skanee Road as you leave L'Anse) to Falls Road (on the right and marked with DNR Public Access and Silver Falls signs). Turn right (south) onto Falls Road and go .7 miles to its end. Silver Falls is about 20 feet straight ahead. The unnamed falls is about 100 yards downstream.

Another waterfall (actually more of a rapids than a falls) and a large pool, which is a popular swimming and fishing hole for local residents, is just around the corner from Silver Falls. To get to them, as you leave the Silver Falls parking area turn left onto the first cross trail and go about 100 yards to its end. A trail from the roadway leads a very short distance to the river.   (Photos, p. 68)

Silver River Falls (#66, p. 67)

Baraga County

UNNAMED FALLS

Silver River, 4 1/2 miles east of L'Anse

We were very surprised to discover these two lovely falls, since they are not marked on any maps or included in any waterfall lists that we have found.

As the first falls sweeps through the forest, it rushes over many layers of dark rock to form a staircase of white water which descends at least 20 feet. Blue-green moss clings to the rough sections of worn, layered stone which line the banks. The occasionally gold-tinged water gradually narrows downstream, where it twists around golden-brown boulders.

About 100 yards upstream, the second falls, like the first, sweeps powerfully through the green surroundings, then creates its own individual beauty. The river divides around a small outcropping of rough stone to form, on the right, cascades of white which descend over layers of rock. The left flow, on the other hand, slides over a long, flat section of rock to create a dark mirror, its smooth surface unbroken until it drops over a section of stone to rejoin the other stream.

When we visited the falls, the area was not posted with any "Private Property" or "No Trespassing Signs." But after our visit, we received a plat book and learned that both are on private property.

Unnamed Falls (#67, p.67)

The Falls River is one of the most beautiful stretches of flowing water anywhere in Michigan. It is only about 10 miles long, but in that short distance drops over 1,000 feet in its rush to Lake Superior. The Falls River completes its journey by running through the town of L'Anse, which makes the falls along the stream very accessible and easy to find. If we had to recommend just one river to visit in all of Michigan, this would be it.

Beginning at Lower Falls and ending at Power Dam Falls, we will describe eight separate falls . But the river is rarely calm and still, and because it continuously tumbles and churns over countless drops along its course, the true number of distinct waterfalls can only be estimated.

70

LOWER FALLS

Falls River, L'Anse

The Lower Falls is composed of two falls separated by a short distance.

Closest to Lake Superior, the first is part of a century-old dam. Calm and smooth water—a rarity on this river—is held behind the dam by a huge concrete divider. The wide river is compressed through a narrow five-foot channel in the center of the dam, then drops 10 feet and slides by and over the uneven surface of the slab stone which lines the riverbed below. Most of this rock—its once-sharp crevasses and edges now softened and smoothly contoured—is above water level, and its blue-gray color accents the crystal-clear water as it rushes by. A short distance downstream, the 50-foot-wide river drops another three feet in a band of white, then rushes on in rapids interrupted by occasional dry patches of rocky ledge which span the river.

The beauty of the second Lower Falls, located upstream from the dam about 100 yards, is typical of the entire river. As the stream drops a total of about 12 feet, the water rushes over so many different levels of rock that it appears to be just a constant splash over a blanket of rough stone. On the left looking upstream, the river drops abruptly, as the water falls directly from the top level to the base of the falls. But on the right, the rock bed eases down to the base of the falls, and in delicate white tendrils the river traces the contour of the stone beneath. The colorful blue-gray stone stretches up to line both banks. One large section makes a convenient viewing platform, and on the opposite bank, another slab peers out from beneath the awning of thick, leafy trees and shrubs that line the river on both sides. Birch trees here stretch toward the sky, their whiteness reflected in the dark pool that extends downstream from the base of the falls.

Directions: See directions to Middle Falls (#71). (Map, p. 75)

MIDDLE FALLS

Falls River, L'Anse

Certain natural vistas quicken your pulse as you try to take in their beauty. The Middle Falls on the Falls River is one of them.

From the Lower Falls the trail traces its way upstream along a high bluff which overlooks the river. Towering pines stand resolutely on the ridge and frame the river with strength and security. When you first see the falls from this height, it looks like a swatch of fluffy wool, its whiteness contrasting sharply with the black rocks and deep greens of the surrounding forest. Upstream, a railroad bridge spans the river, and from that point, churning white water ducks and bobs downstream about 100 yards to the falls.

Though the river drops a total of 25 feet here, it does so only a few feet at a time. The main section of falls divides, leaving a large section of rough stone in mid-stream to be covered with the uncompromising greens of thick moss and small ferns. The green is wrapped in a white, watery embrace as the river descends in a double staircase along both sides of the isolated slab.

It doesn't get any better than this.

Directions to Lower Falls and Middle Falls: As you enter L'Anse from the south on US-41, turn right, onto Broad Street (just past a tourist information center on the right). Follow Broad Street approximately .6 miles into downtown L'Anse to the blinker light at Main Street. Turn left onto Main Street and go about three blocks, just past a large Celotex Corporation building on the left, to the Falls River. Do not cross the river, but turn left and park next to it. The trail to the falls begins upstream, just outside the fence around the Celotex Corporation's building. (Map, p. 75)

Middle Falls

72

UNNAMED FALLS
Falls River, L'Anse

About 200 yards upstream from the US-41 bridge over the Falls River west of L'Anse, a beautiful unnamed falls makes a slow 12-foot descent over flat ledges of black rock. A good view of the falls comes from a railroad bridge downstream.

From there, the scene looks like a terraced hillside that has been flooded by a sudden cloudburst. In scattered sections, the 25-foot-wide river drops a foot or two at a time, then flattens out to a shallow, smooth pool before making one more small drop. A banner of thick ferns which covers a dry section of rock in the middle of the falls waves in the breeze, and pine branches sweep down from both banks in an attempt to reach the refreshing water below. A pool that stretches downstream from the falls gives the river a rest from its constant activity.

Directions: As you cross the Falls River on US-41 on the west side of L'Anse, look south and you will see the falls about 200 yards upstream. Park off the road in the bridge area and walk up the east side of the river to the falls.

(Map, p. 75)

73

UPPER FALLS
Falls River, L'Anse

The Falls River here narrows to about 20 feet, then cascades over black rock in a 12-foot drop. On the far left as you look upstream, a small flow is separated from the main falls by a section of dry stone dotted with a few wisps of grass. On the right, the river divides into two mirror-image sections as the water cascades over several uneven drops. After the water has descended in a rush of white, it foams out from the base of the falls into a small pool downstream. Although the current is still strong in this pool, some daring local residents use it as a swimming hole. They dive and disappear into the foaming water, then resurface a few yards downstream.

Directions: From US-41 about 1.5 miles south of L'Anse, turn west onto Power Dam Road and go approximately .6 miles (across the railroad tracks) to East River Road. Turn right (north) onto East River Road and go approximately a mile to where the road turns right (east) and crosses the railroad tracks. Park your car on the side of the road before this turn and walk on a trail road which continues north from this point. About 100 feet down this trail road a walking trail heads left. Take that short trail to the falls.

(Map, p. 75)

Unnamed Falls (p. 72)

Power House Falls (p. 74)

POWER HOUSE FALLS (2 Falls)

Falls River, 1 mile south of L'Anse

For reasons unknown, these beautiful falls have escaped the notice of all but a few people who live in the area.

A five-minute walk down an overgrown two-track leads to a view of a long-abandoned brick power house, which towers over the Falls River. A beautiful border of overhanging maple and pine branches on the opposite bank contrasts with the earth tones of the building, and to the right of the structure, a sparkling 30-foot-wide falls (which we'll refer to as Powerhouse Falls to distinguish it from the second falls upstream) pours over a rock ledge. The river makes several drops behind and around the side of the building before plunging 13 feet in a mass of white foaming water. An opening beneath the powerhouse arches above the surface of the river, and the water there disappears into its blackness. At the base of the falls the river gathers in a wide pool, then continues downstream in an extensive series of rapids.

Upstream, several sections of small drops delicately link Powerhouse Falls with the second forgotten beauty, a large falls which drops about seven feet. The white rush of water there divides around a section of rock, its moist surface dusted with moss and clinging thin grass.

Directions: From US-41 about 1.5 miles south of L'Anse turn west onto Power Dam Road and go approximately .7 miles (across a railroad track and past East River Road, on the right) to a trail road on the right. Turn right (north) onto this trail road and park. A gate blocks further vehicle access and you must walk the trail about a quarter of a mile through a former county park to the old power-house and the falls.   (Photo, p. 73)

75

POWER DAM FALLS

Falls River, 1 1/2 miles south of L'Anse

The Falls River here is interrupted by a dam—built across the entire river right on the falls—and the forgotten remnants of a sluiceway which once carried water to the powerhouse below. Only a small falls remains as the river courses under the dam and over a large section of smooth rock on the opposite bank. Any water which rises much above that section of stone is guided on the proper course by a concrete wall. In the middle of the river just below the dam, a section

Keweenaw Bay

US-41

LOWER &
MIDDLE FALLS

L'Anse

Tourist Information
Center

UNNAMED FALLS

UPPER FALLS

POWER HOUSE FALLS

POWER DAM FALLS

Power Dam Rd.

US-41

N

Miles

0   1/2   1

of rusted steel pipe and a slab of concrete lie abandoned to constant erosion by the elements.

Downstream, the river stretches into a large pool, then churns into rapids once again. Also from this dam downstream to the mouth of the river is a very popular trout-fishing area.

Directions: From US-41 about 1.5 miles south of L'Anse turn west onto Power Dam Road and go approximately one mile to the dam site.

DAULT'S FALLS

Dault's Creek, 3 miles southeast of L'Anse

There is no formal trail to Dault's Falls, so you must "bushwack it" for about 10 minutes through 300 yards of forest to get to the banks of Dault's Creek and the falls. The effort is worth it.

The creek's 20-foot total fall here begins with a small drop into two small pools bordered by heavy boulders spattered with light-green moss. The water then slides over smooth stone colored with a mixture of browns and cool-gray. Huge sections of shale edge the falls, but the banks downstream flatten into large soft-green patches of grass. The crystal-clear pools invite wading, and the swiftness of the creek suggests a nice area to try for brook trout.

Directions: On US-41 go south from L'Anse approximately 2.5 miles to Herman Road. Turn left (east) onto Herman Road and go about .8 miles (bearing south) to the trail to the falls, on the right (west). The trail begins directly across the road from a driveway which leads to a house.

Dault's Creek is only about 300 yards from the main road, and there is a well-defined path through the ditch on Herman Road. But the route through the woods is difficult, and we advise you to use caution. We used a compass to help keep us on a straight line to the river and tied red cloth strips to tree limbs to mark a return trail.

77

OGEMAW FALLS

Ogemaw Creek, 7 miles southwest of L'Anse

78

PLUMBAGO FALLS

Plumbago Creek, 8 miles southwest of L'Anse

These two falls are in a remote location, and we were unable to find them during our trips to the area.

UPPER SILVER FALLS

2 miles northeast of Herman

This falls is not accessible to the public, as the trail to it passes through private property after leaving the main road.

TIOGA FALLS
(Also known as Tioga Gorge Falls)

Tioga River, 4 miles northwest of Nestoria

We would not recommend attempting to reach this falls unless conditions are dry. On three separate occasions we tried to drive the trail road to the falls, but each time the road was impassable. We therefore are unable to provide details about the falls.

Directions: On M-28/US-41 drive west from Nestoria approximately 4.5 miles to a trail road on the right (north). The falls is approximately 1 3/4 miles down this trail road.

UNNAMED FALLS

Tioga River, 3 1/2 miles west of Nestoria

As the Tioga River runs through a grassy roadside park, the gold-tinged water falls 10 feet in short drops past huge dark-brown boulders strewn in its course. A wood footbridge crosses the river just downstream from the main section of falls. Facilities at the park include picnic tables, grills and restrooms.

Directions: On M-28/US-41 go west from Nestoria approximately 3.5 miles to a roadside park on the left (south).

Baraga County

82

CANYON FALLS
(Also known as Bacco Falls)

83

UNNAMED FALLS

84

UPPER FALLS

Sturgeon River, 1 1/2 miles south of Alberta

The trail to these three falls penetrates some of the thickest sections of forest in the county. The only visible touch by

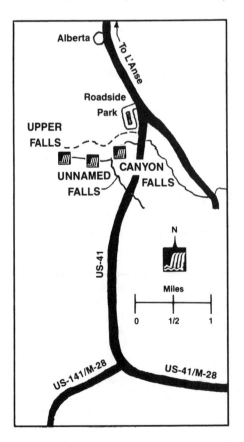

man along the route is a rail fence which runs along one bank of the river. But if you look over this slight intrusion to the opposite bank, there is nothing else to suggest that this is not what the area would have looked like hundreds of years ago.

The trail to the falls begins at the Canyon Falls Roadside Park. After a quarter of a mile, the path reaches the Sturgeon River, then turns to follow the banks downstream. The river here forms a series of rapids, plus a few scattered miniature falls, then quickens its pace as it nears a canyon ahead.

Canyon Falls, the first falls, drops straight into the mouth of this canyon. The smooth ledge at the top of the falls breaks away into a zig-zag pattern as the white rush of water spills downward about 15 feet over a few rock layers, then plunges into a small pool. Black shadows, which run down the length of the falls, contrast with the golden hues of the rock above, and pale-green moss clings in patches to the smooth rock surfaces. As the walls of the far bank rise steeply, they leave a few narrow ledges striped with green growth. Across the falls, the power of the water has washed a hollow into the rock.

The wood fence which has bordered the river stops at a wall of stone to the right of the falls, and it appears as though the trail, too, ends there. The trail, however, picks up again at the back side of the boulder. Just beyond this rock, look back for another outstanding view of Canyon Falls, gently framed by the drooping branches of soft pines.

The trail then follows the river's high banks along the length of what many have called the Grand Canyon of the Upper Peninsula. Thick stands of pine and fir top the moss-covered walls of stone along the route, and the air is thick with the smell of balsam.

About halfway between Canyon Falls and Upper Falls is an easy-to-miss small unnamed falls. If you pass it as you continue downstream (as we did) look for it on the return trip. Looking upstream it will appear as a distant eight-foot drop of white framed entirely by the powerful greens of the surrounding forest.

The river continues its rough course through the bottom of the canyon to Upper Falls. There, the 20-foot-wide river slides nearly 30 feet over a large chute of smooth black rock, then splits just before it falls. The section of stream nearest the trail drops in several long stages, and the flow along the opposite bank is screened from view as it drops out of sight behind a thick stone shelf in the center of the river.

Although the falls are beautiful in their own right, the canyon adds an atmosphere of powerful wildness. Guarded by the thickness of the pine forests and the strength of the canyon walls, these three falls will remain a constant in an ever-changing world.

Directions: On US-41 go south from Alberta approximately 1.5 miles to the Canyon Falls Roadside Park, on the right (west). Facilities at the park include toilets, water and picnic tables.

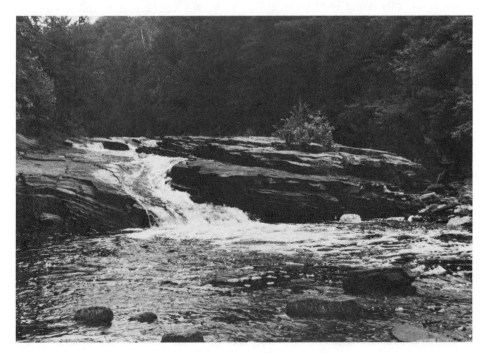

Upper Falls

TIBBETS FALLS

Sturgeon River, 4 1/2 miles northwest of Covington

Thin fingers of rock extend from the banks of the Sturgeon River to create Tibbets Falls. These unusual projections—which sometimes reach to the center of the 50-foot-wide river—rise above the surface, and each forces the water to make a short drop before running against the next section of rock. Dozens of these narrow strips of rock create drops ranging from a few inches to three or four feet.

Directions: On US-141/M-28 go approximately two miles west of Covington to Plains Road. Turn right (north) onto the blacktop road and go a little more than three miles to the Sturgeon River. Cross the river and continue on Plains Road (as it bears left) a short distance to where it bears sharply right (north). At that point leave Plains Road (At one time a sign pointed the way to the falls, but now only a brown post remains.) and continue straight ahead on a trail road approximately .2 miles to a fork. Take the

left fork and go about a half mile to the falls. The trail road ends just below the falls, and there is room to easily turn a truck or car around. In wet weather this trail road may not be passable in a car.

Tibbets Falls

BARAGA COUNTY DAM SITES

2-D
Prickett Falls Dam
Sturgeon River, 10 miles southwest of L'Anse

There are no waterfalls in this area. You can see the dam from your vehicle but cannot get any closer because all of the surrounding land is posted, "No Trespassing."

Eric's Falls (p. 63)

Agate Falls (p.112)

Schweitzer Falls, upper part (p. 32)

Middle Falls, Falls River (p. 71)

Misicot Falls (p. 168)

Ocqueoc Falls (p. 178)

Silver River Falls (p. 106)

Black Slate Falls (p. 65)

Upper Unnamed Falls, Silver River (p. 67)

Bonanza Falls (p. 62)

Munising Falls (p. 13)

Big Falls (p. 62)

HOUGHTON COUNTY

Nature has blessed Houghton County, both above and below the ground.

This is the heart of the Copper Country. Copper deposits first brought Houghton County to the attention of the world and in turn brought immigrants from around the world to work the area's mines. The frenzied activity here during the mid- to late-1800s rivaled (some say surpassed) that of the more publicized and romanticized California Gold Rush.

Some of the world's purest copper ore was mined here, and at the center of the boom was the town of Calumet, then called Red Jacket. The area, which in the late 1800s supported a population of nearly 50,000, was so prosperous that it literally had more money than it knew what to do with. So the community decided to construct (among other things, such as a 16,000-volume library and the state's first concrete streets) an opera house that would match nearly any other in the country. In 1900 the 1,100-seat Calumet Theatre—complete with ultra-modern electric lighting, steam heat and indoor lavatories—opened as America's first such municipally owned facility. Over the next several years some of the period's most famous performers, including Sarah Bernhardt and Lillian Russell, took the stage there. The theatre declined with the area's copper industry but in 1974 was restored to its original beauty and reopened to the public. Visitors today can take a self-guided tour or attend a wide variety of scheduled plays and concerts.

Calumet's population now numbers only about 1,000, but the memory of the copper boom is kept alive in an intriguing mixture of tours, relics and museums scattered throughout the county. Calumet's Coppertown, U.S.A. museum and visitor center, for example, is an excellent place to get a thorough introduction to both the history of copper mining in the area and the people whose lives were affected by the changing currents of that industry. Only about five miles south on M-26 at Lake Linden is the Houghton County Historical Museum. That three-story building, once the main office of the Calumet and Hecla Mining Company, is packed with historical artifacts from the entire Keweenaw Peninsula.

Perhaps the most vivid symbol of the power and importance of copper mining in the Keweenaw Peninsula is the Quincy Mine Hoist, the largest piece of machinery of its kind ever used anywhere in the world. In a building next to Quincy Shaft House No. 2, which towers over Hancock on a hill on the north, visitors can examine the giant equipment, which once lifted 10-ton loads of copper ore at speeds of over 36 miles per hour.

A few copper mines—such as the Arcadian Mine, also located just outside Hancock—remain open to the public for tours. The thrilling experience of walking beneath the earth in an actual copper mine cannot be duplicated anywhere else. The past truly does come to life, and the ghostly echoes of long-ago miners linger in your mind as you reach to touch the cold stone surrounding you. In rock piles around many of the area's long-abandoned mines, it's still possible to find pieces of copper ore.

Many areas throughout the county, in fact, are potential treasure troves for rockhounds. Agate hunters equipped with a good eye and persistence can add many specimens to their collections from the county's Lake Superior shoreline. Isle Royale National Park is also good for rock hunting. Though officially part of Keweenaw County, the island's mainland headquarters is at Houghton, from which boats to the park leave daily throughout the summer season. Another can't-miss spot for anyone even mildly interested in minerals, gems and rocks is the 30,000-specimen A.W. Seamen Mineralogical Museum, which is housed at the Michigan Technological University at Houghton.

That school, which opened in 1886 as the Michigan College of Mines, is one of two seats of higher learning which are legacies of the copper mining industry. The other is Suomi College. Founded at Hancock in 1896 by the large population of Finnish immigrants who had come to the U.P. to work the copper mines, the school is the only Finnish insitute of higher learning in the United States.

The two sister cities, Houghton and Hancock, are connected by one of the most unique bridges in the state. The entire double-deck span, which has a four-lane highway on its upper level and a railroad track on its lower level, can be raised to allow ships to navigate through on the Portage Canal below. That waterway, which runs through the peninsula from Lake Superior to Keweenaw Bay, is itself unique in that it was largely man-made (again, to service the copper industry) and when completed in effect changed the Keweenaw Peninsula technically into the Keweenaw "Island."

And finally, a description of Houghton County would be incomplete without mention of one of its most famous native sons, George Gipp, an All-American college football player who died of pneumonia during his senior year at Notre Dame. Immortalized by the now-famous saying, "Win one for the Gipper," the Laurium native is remembered in his home town by a street-corner memorial and Gipp Memorial Recreation Park.

For more specific information about Houghton County and its attractions you may contact:

Department of Natural Resources
Calumet Field Office
M-26
Calumet MI 49913

Ottawa National Forest
Kenton District Ranger
Kenton MI 49943

Department of Natural Resources
Twin Lakes Field Office
RR1, Box 234
Toivola MI 49965

Superintendent
Isle Royale National Park
Houghton MI 49931

Houghton County Historical Museum
    Society
Highway M-26
Lake Linden MI 49945

Upper Peninsula Travel and Recreation
    Association
P.O. Box 400
Iron Mountain MI 49801

STURGEON FALLS

Sturgeon River, 10 miles northeast of Sidnaw

As the Sturgeon River courses through the bottom of the deepest valley in Michigan, it creates Sturgeon Falls. This is a powerful river—as much as 78,000 gallons of water per minute rush over the falls—and its scenic beauty is unparalleled.

To see the falls, you must hike to the bottom of the valley. That three-quarter-mile walk is one of the hardest and also most beautiful we have taken to a Michigan waterfall. As the trail approaches the river, it is still far up the hillside with commanding views over the wide expanse of river and wilderness. From there the trees below look like a cushion that will absorb anything that might intrude. The scattered tops of a few towering pines stretch above the rest of the forest to form dark-green conical silhouettes against the blue sky.

The trail then drops to the banks above an upper falls, a three-foot-high band of white water which stretches 150 feet from bank to bank. To the left of this falls are several small drops, but most of the river falls over the wide, small step. The river here doesn't seem too overpowering, but a glance downstream at huge piles of brush and debris left stranded high on the banks is a vivid reminder of roaring spring currents. Below the falls the river creates a rapids as it passes over countless stones and boulders in midstream.

About 100 feet downstream from that rapids, the river begins to contract to flow through a narrow gorge it has cut into the underlying rock. The river is then forced to concentrate its power as it presses into the six-foot-wide, 15-foot-long chute. At the end of the stone channel the power is suddenly released, as a curtain of water bursts out and over a layer of rock to fall about 30 feet into a riling mass of foam below.

An outstanding view of this section of the falls comes from a red rock bank nearly 40 feet above the river. On the opposite bank, heavy tree branches effectively cut out the sunlight. As a result, the boulders which line the banks above and below the falls are padded with a thick layer of emerald-green moss. Downstream, small sections of stones litter the river to create splotches of white in the slate-colored water. Sections of red sand banks spill into the river, and the the forested hills of the valley beyond rise up toward the sky.

Directions: From M-28 approximately one mile west of the Baraga/Houghton County line turn north onto USFS-191 (marked by a sign pointing to the Sturgeon River Campground.) Go approximately two miles on USFS-191 to a fork. Go right, continuing on USFS-191 (and following the signs to Sturgeon River Campground) for about 3.6 miles to the Sturgeon River. (As you cross the river, you will see the Sturgeon River Campground on the left.) Continue on USFS-191 for approximately six more miles to USFS-193, just past where USFS-191 bears sharply right. (A sign here points left to the falls.) Turn left (northwest) onto USFS-193 and go a mile to a trailroad on the left (also marked with a sign) that leads to the falls. Turn left (south) and go about a half mile to the parking area. During wet weather you may have to walk the road from USFS-193.

From the parking area an old four-wheel-drive trail leads down the hill toward the river. Follow that trail to the bottom of the hill, then head upstream approximately a half mile to the falls. As you start upstream, the trail is still high above the river, which you can see below. The trail then leaves the river before circling back to a point just above the main falls.

Sturgeon Falls

Houghton County

JUMBO FALLS

Jumbo River, 2 1/4 miles southwest of Kenton

Jumbo Falls is a series of rapids that extend from a parking area to about a quarter of a mile downstream. There is no trail, and the only way to see the falls is to walk along the riverbanks through the thick surrounding forest. Just below the first drop, the remains of a wooden bridge protrude from the shady banks. Soft, green grass borders the 15-foot-wide river as it passes over numerous short drops and rapids. Many small pools and fallen logs scattered along the swift flow suggest the makings of a fine trout stream.

Directions: From M-28 approximately two miles west of Kenton turn left (south) onto Golden Glow Road and go about 1.5 miles to England Road. Turn left (east) onto England Road and go about .2 miles east to a fork. Go right (south) on the main road a little less than one mile to

Jumbo Creek. (As you near the river you will be in an area that was once a gravel pit.) Park near the river and look for the remains of an old wooden bridge. The rapids start at the old wooden bridge and continue downstream for about a quarter of a mile.

88

SPARROW RAPIDS

East Branch Ontonagon River, 3 miles northwest of Kenton

As its name indicates, Sparrow Rapids is more of a rapids than a waterfall. An upper rapids drops about a foot as it slides over dark sheets of rock, and the river then descends another five feet in a series of rapids. The swift, shallow flow, with a scattering of small pools, makes the river here a good location for fishing.

These rapids run by the Sparrow Rapids USFS Campground. Overnight or day-use facilities there include picnic ta-

bles, fire rings, toilets and water.

Directions: From M-28 just east of Kenton turn north onto FH-16 and go approximately .2 miles to USFS-207. Turn left (west) onto USFS-207 and go 3.2 miles to Sparrow Rapids Campground. Turn left into the campground and park on the right. From the small parking area a sign points the way, to the right, to the trail which leads to steps down a hill about 50 feet to the rapids.

89

ONION FALLS

Onion Creek, 6 1/2 miles northeast of Trout Creek

Because of the remoteness of Onion
Falls and the lack of marked trails to it,
we would not recommend a visit.

90

VISTA FALLS

North Branch Sturgeon River, 6 miles southwest of Nisula

We were unable to find Vista Falls,
which are located approximately one mile
south of USFS-449 and six miles southwest of Nisula. We made several trips up
and down USFS-449 and could not find a
trail which led to this falls. We did try
three short trails which led south from

USFS-449 into a large clear-cut area.
However, the trails were bulldozed shut
there and did not appear to continue any
farther.

Therefore, we do not recommend travel
to Vista Falls without current, reliable directions.

WEST BRANCH STURGEON FALLS
West Branch Sturgeon River, 3 miles south of Nisula

Because of poor trail conditions and steep hills in this remote area, we would recommend entering in a four-wheel-drive vehicle only, unless conditions are very dry. We attempted to visit this falls after periods of heavy rain and only made it about a half mile down the trail in our two-wheel-drive vehicle.

Directions: On M-38 go a little less than a mile west of Nisula to USFS-448 (the first road on the left). Turn left (south) onto USFS-448 and go about 2.9 miles to a two-track trail on the left. (You will cross only one bridge on the way to this trail. If you come to a second bridge you've gone too far.) The falls is approximately one mile down the two-track, then about 200 yards through the woods on the right.

WYANDOTTE FALLS
Misery River, 1 1/2 miles southwest of Twin Lakes

Only about 250 yards from a parking area the 12-foot-wide Misery River moves slowly out from the forest to fall in several stages over rough, black stone. In the first section, white water drops about 10 feet as it fans down the dark rock, then disappears behind large boulders in the streambed. After forming a small, hidden pool behind these moss-covered rocks, the stream gradually drops another 10 feet. A soft cushion of moss covers most of the rock surfaces near the water, and pale-green ferns and light grasses creep from the banks toward the water's edge. The forest here is in a damp low-lying area. Moss covers the tree bark, and thick ferns sprout from the earth.

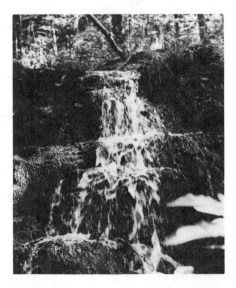

Houghton County

RIPLEY FALLS

Ripley Creek, Ripley

Ripley Falls is very pretty in the spring or after a heavy rain, but in the summer it is nearly dry. The small stream drops a total of 25 feet as it runs past huge dark-brown rocks which divide the falls into two sections. The area near the falls is deeply shaded by thick woods.

Directions: From US-41 in Hancock, just after crossing the lift bridge from Houghton, turn right (east) onto M-26 and go less than a mile to Ripley. In Ripley watch for an old brick school building up a hill on the left. Just past that school turn left (north) onto Arcadia Street and go two blocks to 3rd Street. Turn left (west) onto 3rd Street and go about a block to where it deadends, just before the creek. Park on the side of the road. The walk to the falls takes only five minutes on a trail which heads upstream to the right.

Directions: Wyandotte Falls is located near Twin Lakes State Park, about 20 miles southwest of Houghton on M-26. Coming from the north on M-26 (just past Twin Lakes State Park on the left and a D.N.R field office on the right) turn right (west) onto Poyhonen Road (a sign points to the Wyandotte Hills Golf Course). Go approximately .8 miles to a parking area on the left. This parking area is just past some old log cabins on the right, which themselves are just past the golf course. The trail to Wyandotte Falls twists through the thick surrounding woods to meet the Misery River about 250 yards from the parking area.

94

UPPER HUNGARIAN FALLS

95, 96 and 97

3 UNNAMED FALLS

98

LOWER HUNGARIAN FALLS

Hungarian Creek, 1 mile west of Hubbell

Upper Hungarian Falls is tucked into the snug confines of a beautiful hardwood forest, and its frosty white water contrasts sharply with the greens of the surrounding trees. As the falls drops about 25 feet over a sheer wall of reddish stone, separate strands of water trace patterns which reach toward its base. The falls is about 10 feet wide, about the same as the river as it continues to wind its way through the forest.

Downstream from Upper Hungarian Falls, the creek slides over the sheer surface of Hungarian Dam. The stream's natural course here was altered to flow through a channel in the dam. But during periods of high water, the river also follows its original path and in doing so creates an unnamed falls just below the dam on the far side of the river. There in the shade of bushes which line the banks, a small stream of water falls softly over a moss-covered five-foot red rock wall whose seams and ledges appear so regular and balanced that it looks handmade.

A trail from the dam area crosses over roots and mossy stones as it follows the riverbanks downstream about 100 yards to a second unnamed falls. There, the river makes a graceful descent of about seven feet, then spreads out into a small pool. A low-lying rock shelf stretches out on both sides, and the falls makes a brief splash over the center of the dark stone. You may have to scramble over a few steep rocks to get the best views of this falls.

Downstream another 250 feet, the river again drops, this time in a sheer 25-foot fall broken only by two sections of rock which thrust forward to touch the center of the flow. This unnamed falls creates a beautiful white focal point in a darkly shaded canyon. Scattered bushes dot the face of the high canyon walls, which extend from both sides of the falls, and dark-green moss clings to cracks in the red stone.

About 400 feet downstream is Lower Hungarian Falls, the most spectacular of the five falls in this area. As you walk along the riverbank near the top of the falls, you are close enough to examine in detail the very gradually terraced rock which the river sweeps across. The river drops about 15 feet in this area, and the water creates a pulsing rhythm of life as it courses over the smooth stone.

To view the entire falls, you must walk along the top of the ridge as it extends out from the falls. (Be extremely careful with children in this area.) Through the trees you can catch glimpses of the white-water terraces, then suddenly the entire river shoots out over the side of the ravine in a magnificent 50-foot-plus drop. The thick forest at the bottom of the ravine hides the base of the falls, but traces of its whiteness come tantalizingly into view as it drops through the greens of the trees. And out over the treetops far below, the azure blue of Torch Lake peeks out from the horizon.

There is little along the route from Upper Hungarian falls to suggest that it will end in such a vista, and the view is all the more breathtaking because it is so totally unexpected.

Directions: From M-26 on the southern outskirts of Hubbell, turn north onto Sixth Street (marked by a golf course sign) and go two blocks to a fork. Take the left fork and follow the road, which becomes gravel, up a hill to a trail on the left that has been closed with piles of dirt. Continue about a quarter of a mile to the second trail road past the dirt piles. Turn left onto this trail and go about .2 miles to a fork.

To get to Upper Hungarian Falls, take the right fork a short distance to an old mill pond area. Park there and walk around the pond upstream about 400 yards to the falls.

To get to the remaining falls, drive back to the fork, turn right and park. The trail follows the riverbank. The first unnamed falls is slightly upstream from the parking area and the other two unnamed falls and Lower Hungarian Falls are downstream. (Photo, p. 96)

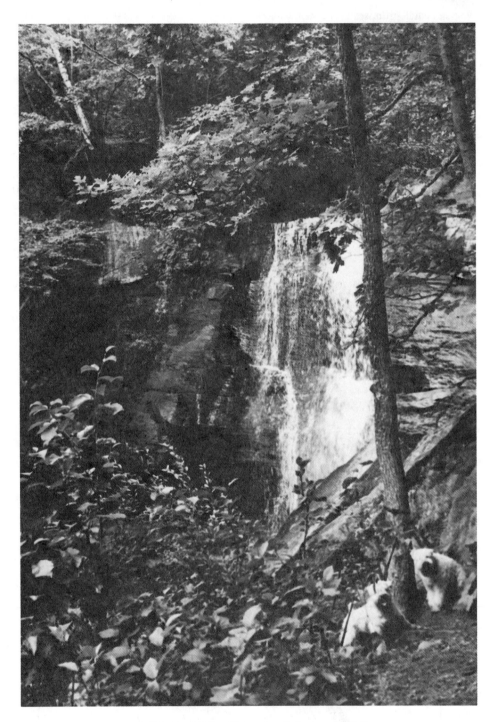

Unnamed Falls, Hungarian Falls area (p. 94)

Houghton County

DOUGLAS HOUGHTON FALLS

Hammell Creek, 1 1/2 miles northwest of Lake Linden

A 10-minute walk along the easy trail to Douglas Houghton Falls leads to beautiful sweeping vistas in all directions from the summit of a towering hill. At the crest, a 10-foot-wide stream meanders through grass-cushioned banks, drops a few feet over ledges of square rocks, then disappears over the side of the hill. As you follow along the top of the hill, a canyon extends outward from the small stream, and it is into it that the water plunges. In a trail of white the creek falls across reddish rocks, clinging to the stone before stretching out from the side of the cliff and plunging nearly 100 feet into the deep canyon below. The canyon walls rise steeply to frame the river with reddish-brown stone.

Barely discernible at the river's edge in the base of the canyon is an entrance to the long-abandoned Douglas Houghton Mine. The dark hole is filling with stone, and it is only a matter of time before all trace of it will have disappeared.

The smooth hilltop—with the surrounding hills and valley stretching out to the horizon, and the dramatic depth of the canyon below—makes an excellent picnic site.

Directions: On M-26 go approximately 1.5 miles from where it turns sharply at a blinker light on the north edge of Lake Linden to a large, well-used parking area on the right. The trail to the falls approaches along the top of a deep canyon, so if you are bringing children, extreme caution is advised.   (Photos, p. 98)

Laurium

Miles

0   1/2   1

DOUGLAS
HOUGHTON
FALLS

M-26

N

Lake Lake Linden

M-26

Hubbell

Torch
Lake

Douglas Houghton Falls, Upper Section (p. 97)

Douglas Houghton Falls (p. 97)

HOUGHTON COUNTY DAM SITES

3-D
REDRIDGE FALLS DAM
Salmon Trout River, 10 miles west of Houghton

There is no waterfall at this site, but the dam, which was completed in 1901, is both interesting and very unusual. Instead of cement and other materials common to the time period, pieces of steel, intricately pieced together, were used to construct the dam.

Directions: From M-26 just west of Houghton, turn west onto Co. Rd. P-554/Houghton Canal Rd., which follows the Portage Ship Canal, and go approximately 4.8 miles to the road which goes to Redridge (marked with a sign). Turn left and drive west on that road about 5.8 miles through Redridge to the dam, on the left just as the road crosses the Salmon Trout River.

4-D
LOWER FALLS DAM
East Branch Ontonagon River, 5 1/2 miles southwest of Sidnaw

There is no visible falls at this location, but the area is very attractive to campers and fishermen. A beautiful USFS campground hugs the shores of the small lake created by the dam. That lake has been stocked with rainbow trout, and the stream below the dam is good for brook trout.

Directions: From M-28 in Sidnaw turn south onto Co. Rd. 161 and go two miles to a gravel road. (A U.S. Forest Service sign there reads, "Lower Dam 4 miles.") Turn right (west) onto the gravel road and go three miles to USFS-139. Turn left (south) onto USFS-139 and go about one mile to the dam and campgrounds.

KEWEENAW COUNTY

Michigan's motto, "If you seek a pleasant peninsula, look about you," is never more apt than when you are standing in Keweenaw County, which comprises the upper two thirds of the beautiful Keweenaw Peninsula. To visitors it seems as if every trail there connects yet another in a long chain of natural attractions.

Brockway Mountain Drive, for example—which twists and turns along the edge of precipitous cliffs from Copper Harbor—is one of the most popular sections of roadway in the entire Upper Peninsula. Built during the Depression, the 9.5-mile stretch of blacktop is the highest above-sea-level roadway between the Alleghanies and the Rockies. People travel hundreds of miles for the pleasure of driving along its curves and hills, especially when the fall color of the thickly forested surrounding hills is at its peak.

If you enjoy wild, unspoiled beauty you won't want to miss Estivant Pines, the last section of privately owned virgin white pine in Michigan. These regal trees, some of which are over 400 years old, were recently saved from the lumberman's saw by the Michigan Nature Association (MNA). Their 200-acre sanctuary, located near Copper Harbor, is open to the public, and as you meander down the trails, your face shaded from the sun by the tangle of branches extending far overhead, it is hard to imagine that the slender trunks of these few beautiful pines once stretched skyward from just about everywhere in the Upper Peninsula.

Isle Royale is another unspoiled wilderness, this one protected by the federal government, which turned Michigan's northernmost parcel of land into a national park. The 134,000-acre island is a nature lover's paradise, with an untouched beauty all its own and a large wildlife population which includes its two most famous inhabitants, moose and wolves. Moose became a part of the island's fauna in 1912 when Lake Superior completely froze and they were able to cross from the mainland. When the lake again froze solid 37 years later, wolves made the same trek. Isle Royale is also a good destination for rock collectors, who can find Michigan's official gemstone, the greenstone, there. Boats to the island leave daily throughout the summer season from both Houghton and Copper Harbor.

Keweenaw County is not without man-made attractions. On the north shore of beautiful Lake Fanny Hooe, for example, stands Fort Wilkins, the only surviving original wooden army fort east of the Mississippi. Built in 1844, the fort was used sporadically for only a few years before it was finally abandoned in 1870. It is now a state park, and visitors can tour the refurbished and refurnished buildings and other large displays that show what army life was like in the mid-1800s.

Not far away, at the tip of a peninsula which juts out into Lake Superior, is Copper Harbor Lighthouse, its picturesque whiteness bordered by the blues and greens of the lake. The lighthouse, which houses an interesting maritime-history museum is accessible only by tour boat.

Keweenaw County also is "copper country," and dozens of long-abandoned copper mines are scattered throughout the area. A few offer guided tours of the dark cavities, whose damp air and empty stillness create an atmosphere so out of place with the former centers of activity and sheer labor. Many of the mines, in fact, gave birth to and nurtured small, secluded communities. When the mines closed, so did the towns. The few buildings left standing in these ghost towns offer only mute testimony to the strength they once had, a strength that was once such an integral part of the Keweenaw Peninsula.

For more specific information about Keweenaw County and its attractions, you may contact:

Keweenaw Tourism Council
Calumet MI 49913

Michigan Nature Association
MNA Business Office
7981 Beard Road
P.O. Box 102
Avoca MI 48006

Superintendent
Isle Royale National Park
Houghton MI 49931

Upper Peninsula Travel and Recreation
  Association
P.O. Box 400
Iron Mountain MI 49801

Eagle River Falls (p. 104)

100

UPPER FALLS

Gratiot River, 3 miles northwest of Ahmeek

101

LOWER FALLS

Gratiot River, 3.5 miles northwest of Ahmeek

The short path to the Upper Falls leads to the crest of a ridge about 40 feet above the Gratiot River, which twists through the trees below. The surrounding forest is very thick, and some trees stretch upward past the cliff edge and trail. Many of the trunks are brushed with flaky, light-green moss which, though it looks like a layer of ashes fragile enough to be blown away in the wind, clings solidly to the bark. The trail follows the river on the ridge, and its proximity to the edge of the cliff can be dangerous, as the conglomerate stone is continuously being worn away by the elements.

The main drop of the Upper Falls, too, runs over a mass of the conglomerate rock so prevalent in the area. As the river gradually drops about 15 feet, the flow rushes over a myriad of small rocks embedded in the stone to create one large section of shallow white water sparkling in the sunlight. The 20-foot-wide river then forms a large section of rapids as it continues downstream.

Though we did not locate the Lower Falls, we believe that the sure way to reach it would be by walking a difficult route downstream. It is possible, as we did, to get down to the river's edge, but there is no formal trail to the Lower Falls. Fallen trees and thick brush made it difficult to follow the riverbank, and we had to stop after a short distance. We then tried to locate the falls by driving to the opposite side of the river. Again we didn't succeed, this time because of active logging in the area.

Directions: From M-26/US-41 just northeast of Ahmeek turn north onto 5 Mile Point Road and go about 2.3 miles to Farmer Block Road. Turn left (west) onto Farmer Block Road and go straight, a little over a mile, to a trail road. Continue on this trail road about a half mile to a gate. Park just before the gate and follow the path, to the left, downhill to the Upper Falls.

UNNAMED FALLS

Silver Creek, 2 miles southwest of Eagle River

When we first tried to find this falls, we followed a map which placed it somewhere between the highway bridge and Lake Superior. Following the river through the woods was a beautiful walk, but we found no waterfalls, only rapids.

Before we left the area, my father, out of curiosity, took a short walk upstream from the bridge. There he found one of the most beautiful small falls in the Upper Peninsula.

To get to it, take a trail which starts on a ridge then drops down to follow the banks of the river upstream. The small river here runs through a high-walled canyon whose sides gradually slope down toward the water. This conglomerate stone is covered by a carpet of bright-green moss whose softness blends with the dark shadows of the forest floor. Thick branches high overhead allow only a dapling of sunlight to reach through, touching here a branch, there a section of water.

In the distance is a slash of bright, white movement. There, the stream drops about 15 feet in a frothy white curtain which splashes over the conglomerate rock. Framed by the deep emerald greens of the surrounding moss and ferns, the tantalizing beauty of this falls has a strong visual impact. The softness of the shaded forest creates an atmosphere of relaxation, and the overall experience is a delight to all the senses.

Directions: From M-26 just south of the village of Eagle River turn west onto 5 Mile Point Road and go approximately 1.7 miles to Silver Creek. Make a U turn before crossing Silver Creek and park on the side of the road. Follow Silver Creek (it runs next to the road for a short distance) upstream approximately a quarter of a mile to the falls. (Photo, p. 104)

EAGLE RIVER FALLS

Eagle River, in the town of Eagle River

Eagle River Falls creates a dramatic welcome to the town of Eagle River. You can see the falls from your car, but you should stop for a longer look.

The falls is on the original site of the Lake Superior Fuse Co., and the remains of a dam still span most of the 60-foot-wide river. (The plant burned in 1957, but the dam was never demolished.) The dam's wooden slats extend what was already a tall falls to a total height of well over 60 feet. In a straight sheet, the copper-colored water drops over the top of the dam. Then its forces scatter as the river rushes headlong over the cracked black rock which forms its steep banks. On the left bank, small tendrils of water trace patterns over the rock and gradually rejoin the powerful current of the main falls as it reaches the bottom of the deep gorge.

Directions: As M-26 enters the village of Eagle River from the south, it crosses an old bridge over the Eagle River. The falls are to the right of the bridge, a short distance upstream. For a leisurely view of the falls, cross over the bridge and park on the right.

(Photo, p. 101) (Map, p. 105)

Unnamed Falls, Silver Creek (p. 103)

JACOBS FALLS

Jacobs Creek, 3 miles northeast of Eagle River

You can see Jacobs Falls from your car, but it also is a a pleasant place to stop, visit and explore. If you look back through the trees from the road, you can see that the falls, though small, has a total drop of about 40 feet. Close to the road, the main section drops about 20 feet in a network of white lines traced over the surface of the rough stone. A border of bare rock keeps the green, bushy woods back from the river. Trails, which run up the sides of the steep rock, lead farther back into the woods upstream. There, mossy banks provide an anchor for cedar trees whose frayed

trunks stretch upward toward the light.

Directions: Go northeast of Eagle River on M-26 approximately three miles to Jacobs Falls, on the right.

105

COPPER FALLS

Owl Creek, 3 miles southwest of Eagle Harbor

Nestled in the deep woods near Eagle Harbor is Copper Falls. An active copper-mining town with the same name once covered an area near the falls, and Copper Creek is said to have passed directly through the mine at one time. The trail to the falls passes a few of the structures that remain in the ghost town.

When we visited in midsummer, the stream was but a bare trickle which fell in a few strands over what appeared to be a seven-foot-high shelf of rock. But when we walked closer, we could see that dec-

ades ago, evidently, a log dam had been constructed on the top of the original shelf of rock. The deep, green shadows of thick, hanging moss outlines the shapes of the logs in the upper portion of the falls.

Downstream from the dam and falls, the tiny flow of water wanders through smooth moss-covered stones which are dappled with sunlight. Ferns, plus small pines that have just begun to take hold, line the banks.

(Continued on p. 106)

SILVER RIVER FALLS

Silver River, 4 1/2 miles east of Eagle Harbor

Silver River Falls begins just downstream from the M-26 bridge. You can't view the falls from your car, but it is a short, easy walk down the banks of the river. And from a distance the stone arches of the bridge form a perfect backdrop to the falls.

The river is at least 15 feet wide here and, in a series of rapids, rushes over the stone bed toward the falls. On one bank, a section of light-brown rock slopes steeply to the water's edge. The opposite side is shrouded in bushes and outstretched tree branches. At the falls, the stream divides to drop about seven feet over a small rock outcropping, then continues as rapids to another sudden drop. The river splits for a second time, and

the rock divider—which remains dry enough to support a layer of wild grasses—is a small island of green in the midst of dark water. After each drop, the river takes a brief respite in a small pool.

Farther downstream, the river narrows to about seven feet and continues on with renewed energy. As we watched it course over a many-terraced section of stone, we were reminded of the fall's name. The water caught the full power of the sun and reflected its light as from one shining block of silver, its sparkling surface sharply contrasting with the deep greens around it. Just past this point, the river cuts a channel into the dark rock and continues through the forest and out of view.

(Photo, p. 84)

COPPER FALLS

(Continued from p. 105)

Directions: As M-26 enters Eagle Harbor from the west it makes a 90-degree turn, to the right (south) at the waterfront. About two blocks farther, just past a motel and restaurant, the highway makes another 90-degree turn, this time left (east). At that point turn south from M-26 onto an unmarked blacktop road (which goes to Eagle River) and go approximately three miles to Owl Creek. Cross Owl Creek and go to the second trail road on the left. (This trail enters the main road at an angle from behind and is fairly easy to miss.) Turn left onto the trail road and go about a half mile to its end. A turnaround there is up a steep hill, so we chose to park at the trail's end and back up a short distance to turn

around when we left. The falls are about 30 feet directly in front of the trail road at its end.

Directions: From Eagle Harbor go east on M-26 about 4.5 miles to the Silver River (just before the point where Brockway Mountain Drive intersects with M-26). Park in the parking area on the side of the road and walk downstream to the falls.

Silver River Falls

MANGANESE FALLS

Manganese Creek, 1 mile southeast of Copper Harbor

The beauty of Manganese Falls is unassuming yet powerful. And it waits patiently for anyone with the time and the inclination to stop by, which is not difficult to do. It is just a few minutes' walk on a trail which runs along the top of a deep gorge. A wooden railing keeps visitors back from the edge, and the tall rock walls completely hide the falls. Then as the trail ends at a viewing area, the sweeping beauty of Manganese Falls comes into sight.

Manganese Creek spills from the top of the gorge, then forms a delicate trail of water as it falls at least 45 feet to the rocky bottom. As the narrow tendrils of water fall, they play hide-and-seek behind the leafy branches which stretch across the narrow canyon. The sheer stone walls are spattered with a pale blue-green moss whose smooth, paper-thin surface forms a soft highlight to the delicacy of the falls. The floor of the small canyon is so

thick with trees and bushes that you can only assume that the creek runs through the bottom of the ravine.

Directions: From the intersection of M-26 and US-41 in Copper Harbor, go east three blocks to the Copper Harbor Community and Visitors Center building on the right. Turn right (south) onto the street immediately past that building and go approximately .7 miles (past the tip of Lake Fanny Hooe, then slightly beyond where the road makes a sharp right turn) to the falls, on the left. The falls are about 100 feet from the main road.

Haven Falls

108

UPPER FALLS

109

LOWER FALLS

Montreal River, 6 miles east of Bete Grise

Because of poor trail conditions due to logging in the area, we were unable to visit these falls, and we would recommend driving this trail during wet weather in a four-wheel-drive vehicle only. Even if you have a four-wheel-drive vehicle you should walk from Smith's Fisheries to the falls, about two miles one way.

Directions: On Bete Grise Rd. go east from Lac LaBelle approximately 2.8 miles to a trail road on the left. Turn left onto the trail road, which will fork immediately. Take the right fork to Smith's Fisheries.

110

HAVEN FALLS

Haven Creek, 1/2 mile west of Lac La Belle

Haven Falls is small, and its perfection gives it the appearance of being man-made. It's also easy to see. The falls is located at the back of a roadside park but is close enough to the parking area to be seen from a car.

As the small creek runs over the side of a rock outcropping, it stretches white tendrils downward to form a perfectly rectangular block of white against a backdrop of dark stone. Just downstream, a small footbridge, which spans the creek, adds an interesting accent to the falls. Trails follow the creek upstream, but they are rather steep.

Facilities at Haven Park, which is a beautiful spot for a picnic, include tables, grills and restrooms.

Directions: From US-41 approximately one mile east of Delaware, turn south onto the road to Lac La Belle. Go approximtely 4.5 miles to Lac La Belle, then turn right and go about a half mile to Haven Park, on the right. The route to the park from US-41 is well-marked with signs.

ONTONAGON COUNTY

Ontonagon County is a paradise for nature lovers, and opportunities for hunting, fishing and other outdoor activities there are almost unlimited. More than 90 percent of the county is forested. Parts of the Ottawa National Forest take up large chunks of the county's acreage, and other sections go to make up the Copper Country State Forest. About half of the Upper Peninsula's largest lake, Lake Gogebic, also lies in Ontonagon County, the other half in Gogebic County, to the south.

But probably the county's most well-known natural attraction is Porcupine Mountains State Park, Michigan's largest. Stretching inland from Lake Superior on the county's northwest corner, the "Porkies," as they are called, cover 58,000 acres (including a few in Gogebic County). The "mountains" vary in elevation from 1,000 to 1,400 feet above the level of Lake Superior, and tucked into the folds of these rolling hills are many hidden lakes.

One of the most beautiful is Lake of the Clouds. To most visitors, this elongated section of azure water appears as a slash of vibrant blue which divides the emerald greens of surrounding trees. But for the lucky few who arrive when weather conditions are just right—no wind and a variety of fluffy clouds scuttling by overhead—the lake takes on an amazing beauty. If you peer down into the valley then, you will see, reflected in the glassy visage of the lake, the ivory clouds drifting lazily by in the blue expanse of sky. On these wondrous occasions it truly is a Lake of the Clouds.

More than 85 miles of trails network the park, including many which probe the back country, and backpacking is popular. (Overnight treks must be registered with the park service.) For a truly exclusive and remote vacation hideaway, some visitors use the park's limited number of trailside cabins, which can only be reached by a long hike. And the trails in the Porkies, plus hundreds of other miles elsewhere throughout the county, aren't limited to just summer activity. Skiing, snowmobiling, and even snowshoeing are among popular winter sports, which benefit greatly from the proximity of Lake Superior.

Lake Superior makes a powerful statement wherever she brushes up against land, and Ontonagon County is no exception. During the winter the lake is responsible not only for the abundance of powdery whiteness which blankets the area, but also mild temperatures compared to those farther inland. During the summer, visitors can wander Superior's beaches in search of agates or simply rest and gaze across her rough expanse to glorious red sunsets.

Man-made attractions in Ontonagon County include Silver City, the ghost of a brief and unusual part of Michigan's past. In 1872 silver was discovered along the Iron and

Little Iron Rivers, and the rush was on. Mines started up along the rivers, and Silver City was founded nearby. But no large pockets of silver were found, and as quickly as the frenzied activity started, it stopped. Four years later the only reminders of the short flurry were tales told 'round a campfire of the undiscovered vein that would rival them all.

The copper-mining boom, too, did not bypass the area. Ontonagon County comprises the westernmost section of the Upper Peninsula's copper range, and it was here that the famous Ontonagon Boulder was hauled from the shores of the Ontonagon River. To area Indians, the estimated ton of nearly pure copper symbolized a manitou, a spirit. To geologists and the copper industry which quickly followed, it represented profit. The Ontonagon Boulder, which eventually found its way to the Smithsonian Institute, was ultimately only a prelude to countless tons of ore that were removed until the rich copper fields were finally and inevitably played out.

The Ontonagon County Historical Museum, in Ontonagon, houses many displays of the area's copper-mining past, and several abandoned mines are scattered throughout the area. One, the Adventure Mine in Greenland, offers guided tours. As we've mentioned in introductions to other counties, a mine tour is an experience you don't want to pass up if you are at all interested in the history of an area.

Another relic of the copper-mining days is the town of Victoria, built near the original site of the Ontonagon Boulder. Like so many Upper Peninsula communities, Victoria lost its spark of life when the copper industry abandoned the area. But unlike other small, almost-forgotten mining towns, Victoria is being brought back to life by a large restoration project aimed at recreating the mid-1800s community as it was at its peak. Old Victoria, as it is called, is already open to the public, and when you walk across its green lawns past blooming lilacs, the past has never been so near.

For more specific information about Ontonagon County and its attractions you may contact:

Forest Supervisor
Ottawa National Forest
Ironwood MI 49938

Lake Gogebic Area Chamber of
    Commerce
Bergland MI 49910

Ontonagon County Chamber of
    Commerce
P.O. Box 266
Ontonagon MI 49953

Ottawa National Forest
Bergland Ranger District
Bergland MI 49910

Porcupine Mountains Wilderness State
    Park
599 M-107
Ontonagon MI 49953

Society for Restoration of Old Victoria,
    Inc.
P.O. Box 43
Rockland MI 49960

Upper Peninsula Travel and Recreation
    Association
P.O. Box 400
Iron Mountain MI 49801

AGATE FALLS

Middle Branch Ontonagon River,
4 miles west of Trout Creek

As the sometimes-steep trail to Agate Falls runs over roots and rocks, the middle branch of the Ontonagon River urges visitors on by repeatedly dropping over dark stone to create a chain of miniature falls. The trail leads to a perfect viewing area at the base of the falls. There, the entire scope of the falls stretches out in front of you, and its beauty is captivating. A cool wind, which usually blows down the length of the river and over the falls, touches the skin with its refreshing purity.

The 80-foot-wide river brushes up against the leafy branches of oaks and maples as it sweeps out of the thick forest to drop over a series of square steps sliced out of stone. Cascades within cascades are created as the water tumbles over the black rock, and a series of soft, white trails fall into a pool below. As the river moves slowly over the small stones which fill the shallow pool, it creates a bubbling rapids, then runs through the forest once again.

The trail to Agate Falls begins (and ends) in the Joseph F. Oravec Roadside Park, which is a perfect spot to rest after viewing these popular falls. Facilities at the park include running water, pit toilets and picnic tables.

Directions: On M-28 go approximately four miles west of Trout Creek to the Joseph F. Oravec Roadside Park, on the left (south) side of road.

BOND FALLS

Middle Branch Ontonagon River, 3 1/2 miles east of Paulding

Bond Falls, which drops in two sections, is one of the most spectacular in the Upper Peninsula.

In a rush of white water, the first drop stretches down the river over flat sections of dark rock. The river widens slightly to about 80 feet and at the center makes an abrupt drop into a small pool, forcing the rest of the falling water to curve around it on both sides. Thick, green grasses brush against the water, and branches from the closest trees bend toward it as it passes. From here, the river curves to the right and disappears behind the trees.

Downstream, the banks are lined with a cement abutment to minimize erosion by the strong-flowing river. Water there continues to rush over flat sections of rock, creating a carpet of white all along the area. The cement abutment ends at a viewing platform, which affords an exciting close-up view of the main section of Bond Falls.

The main falls is breathtaking. The water drops nearly 50 feet in a series of step-like drops. The squared-off rock stairs are scattered haphazardly in many different layers, which causes the water to bounce off their flat tops in a complicated pattern of white streams. When viewed from the front, a small grass- and tree-covered island backed by a small section of rock divides the falls into two unequal sections. From the base, the water flows past a scattering of huge rocks, which have fallen from the cliff, to form a large pool which circles out from the falls.

From there the river divides and continues its travels through the shadowed forest. Excellent views of the falls come from two wooden bridges, one spanning each section of the stream.

Facilities near the parking area include picnic tables and a playground for children.

Directions: From US-45 in Paulding turn east onto Bond Falls Road and go about 3.2 miles to a parking area (on both sides of the road) above the falls. Cement-block stepping stones span the river, which is just in front of the parking area, and you can view the falls, which begin just downstream from the blocks, from either bank.

At the beginning of the trail a sign warns of the strength of the river and urges caution. Stick to the paths on shore, as the rocks near and in the river are very slippery. Also, swimming and wading are not allowed.

ROCK BLUFF FALLS

Bluff Creek, 1 1/2 miles south of Paulding

We were unable to locate this waterfall. After rechecking our topographical maps at home, we concluded that this falls is marked incorrectly on some maps, which caused us to look in the wrong area for this falls.

114

LITTLE FALLS

Middle Branch Ontonagon River, 4 1/2 miles southwest of Paulding

Though there is no formal trail, it is an easy 30-foot walk under towering pines and past patches of feathery ferns and tangles of blackberry bushes to the falls. There, the 30-foot-wide river drops four feet over sections of black rocks, creating small areas of copper color as the water rushes over the stone. The banks are grassy in most spots, with some underbrush touching the river in others. If you look downstream through the trees you can see the river as it empties into the Bond Falls Basin.

Directions: Go approximately three miles south of Paulding on US-45 to USFS-172. Turn left (east) onto USFS-172 and go about 3.7 miles to USFS-171, on the right, marked by a "171" written on a brown post. At that point make a *U* turn and head back west on USFS-172. There will be three trails on the right, within .2 miles from the point that you made the *U* turn. Turn right (north) onto the third trail and go about 1.7 miles to the falls, just off the road on the right.

WOLVERINE FALLS

Cisco Branch Ontonagon River, 8 miles west of Paulding

There are conflicting reports whether (1) these falls even exist and (2) if they do, where they are located. We attempted to find the falls, but a sudden thunderstorm persuaded us to turn back. Though we can vouch for the beauty of the area, we do not recommend visiting this falls.

116

18 MILE RAPIDS

South Branch Ontonagon River, 5 1/2 miles south of Ewen

The road to this rapids is on private property.

117

FLANNIGAN RAPIDS

South Branch Ontonagon River, 5 miles north of Ewen

No roads or walking trails lead from main roads to this rapids, and we do not recommend travel into this remote area.

Before you consider taking a trip into any such wilderness areas, we would suggest contacting the U.S. Forest Service or the closest DNR office.

SANDSTONE RAPIDS

Skranton Creek, 9 miles north of Ewen

We found no roads or trails that led to this rapids and would not recommend travel to this area.

THREE RAPIDS FALLS

Middle Branch Ontonagon River, 7 miles northeast of Bruce Crossing

Like most rapids in Ontonagon County, Three Rapids Falls has no access roads or trails and is located on private property in a wilderness area.

Cascade Falls

120

O-KUN-DE-KUN FALLS

(Also known as Baltimore Falls)

Baltimore River, 8 miles north of Bruce Crossing

There is no access trail to this falls, and
we would not recommend travel into the
area.

121

IRISH RAPIDS

Ontonagon River, 3 miles northwest of Rockland

122

GRAND RAPIDS

Ontonagon River, 5 miles northwest of Rockland

We attempted to reach both rapids from
US-45 northwest of Rockland. But trails
leading to the rapids either had cables strung across them or were posted as no-
trespassing areas.

123

CASCADE FALLS

Cascade Creek, 7 miles northeast of Bergland

There are two trails to Cascade Falls,
the Twin Peaks Route and the Valley
Route. The Twin Peaks trail is longer, but
more scenic. We took the valley trail,
which is lower and easier, although it
does involve a few steep climbs. Ferns
line the path as it laces its way through the heavy woods about a mile to the edge
of Cascade Creek. Upstream, huge spire-
shaped pines, which border the small
river, stretch their green darkness against
the sky. And wildflowers—including wild

(Continued on p. 118)

124

DERBY FALLS

Derby Creek, 3 1/2 miles northeast of Bergland

125

HIDDEN FALLS

Unnamed Creek, 3 1/2 miles north of Bergland

Though the general locations of both falls are included in waterfall lists and a tourist brochure, no one we talked to in the local area knew their specific locations.

CASCADE FALLS
(Continued from p. 117)

(Continued from p. 117)

roses, which grow along the riverbanks—are scattered throughout the area.

The river here is about 15 feet wide, and as it begins its 20-foot descent, it cuts through a section of bedrock to leave a steep wall for its right bank. As the stream spreads out to the left, it drops five feet, then twists around and over several sections of rock stranded in midstream. Numerous still pools and swirling eddies in this area are good for trout fishing or simply wading on a hot afternoon.

Directions: On M-28 go east of Bergland 1.2 miles to USFS-222. Turn left (north) onto USFS-222 and go approximately seven miles (as the road gradually bears northeast) to USFS-831. (Just before this intersection is a "Cascade Falls" sign.) Turn right (east) onto USFS 831 and go .3 miles to the parking area and the start of both trails, which are clearly marked by signs along their respective routes.

126

DEER CREEK FALLS

Deer Creek, 7 miles northwest of Bergland

127

RAPID RIVER FALLS

Rapid River, 5 miles northwest of Bergland

Both falls are in an active logging area on privately owned land criss-crossed by many new roads not shown on maps. We do not recommend travel to these falls.

Bonanza Falls (p. 121)

LITTLE TRAP FALLS

Anderson Creek, 11 miles south of Silver City

Though there is no formal trail, it's a short walk through the woods to Anderson Creek and the falls. The small river is nestled in the base of a dark, shaded ravine brightened here and there by shafts of sunlight which filter through the overhanging branches. The shallow water drops a total of about six feet over rounded stones cushioned with thick, green moss.

Directions: From M-107 approximately a quarter mile east of Silver City turn south onto M-64 and go about 9 miles to the intersection with Old 64. Stay left and

go south about 1.5 miles on Old 64 to where it curves left. A short distance farther, the road curves back to the right and, as it straightens out, starts up a hill. Continue up the hill to the first yellow "Caution Pipeline" sign on the right. At that point make a *U* turn and park on the side of the road.

Head into the woods on the right (east) and go about 300 yards to the third ravine. There is no trail, so don't attempt the walk without a compass and be sure to mark a trail for the trip out. The creek is at the bottom of the third ravine, and the falls are slightly downstream.

PEWABECK FALLS

Little Iron River, 1 1/2 miles southwest of Silver City

Directions: From Silver City go west on M-107 (across the Little Iron River at one mile) about 1.5 miles to a trail road on the left. We were not able to reach this falls because the road was rutted and deep with mud. Before attempting to

reach Pewabeck Falls, we suggest that you ask for the latest trail conditions at the grocery store in Silver City. The store owner told us that the road is usually in too bad a condition for anything but a four-wheel-drive vehicle.

BONANZA FALLS
(Also known as Greenwood Falls)

Big Iron River, 1 mile south of Silver City

All of our preliminary research had indicated that there was one waterfall in this section of the Big Iron River, so we were surprised and pleased to discover two falls about 200 yards apart.

The rocks which line the riverbed here are some of the most unusual we've seen. They appear to be composed of dozens of layers—which vary in thickness from millimeters to an inch, each colored a subtly different shade of brown—compressed together. As far as the eye can see both upstream and downstream, sections of the banded stone thrust at an angle out of the bed to form a network of walkways across the 130-foot-wide river. From behind, the water cuts away at the diversions as it winds its way through them.

A short distance directly in front of the parking area, the first falls drops about 10 feet through a channel lined with this soft, worn rock. When we visited in July, not much water was flowing over the falls into the deep pool of slow-moving water below. Downstream about 200 yards, the second falls drops much like the first but only a total of about three feet.

These falls would be worth a visit during just about all water conditions. At low levels, more of the unusual jutting rocks are exposed, and during high water the size of the falls increases dramatically.

Directions: From M-107 about a quarter of a mile east of Silver City turn south onto M-64 and go about one mile to a trail road on the right. Turn right (west) onto the trail and go to a parking area just off the highway. From there, in dry weather you can drive the .1 mile to the river; in wet conditions, you may have to walk. **(Photo, p. 119)**

NONESUCH FALLS

Little Iron River, 5 miles southwest of Silver City

Nonesuch Falls begins with a modest one-foot drop between rough stone banks. The main falls then divides into two separate flows separated by dry rock in the center. Each of the white streams slides 12 feet over the smooth face of the chocolate-colored stone into a pool below. From that seven-foot-deep pool the river slowly meanders out of sight behind a covering of trees.

The thick forest here brushes up against the banks of the 15-foot-wide river, and just above the falls are the remains of the old Nonesuch Mine.

Directions: On M-107 go west from Silver City about 2.5 miles to South Boundary Road. Turn left (south) onto South Boundary Road and go about 4.3 miles. Near this point, where South Boundary Road bears right, go straight ahead on a narrow gravel road approximately .8 miles to the falls.

When we visited, the road was bad, and we were able to drive only about halfway to the falls. The road gave out at a large mudhole surrounded by a large,

swampy field, so we parked our truck and continued on foot another 10 minutes to the falls.

Nonesuch Falls

Numerous named and unnamed waterfalls are located within the boundaries of Porcupine Mountains State Park. The walks to them range from a few feet to lengthy hikes deep into the park's interior. A small portion of the park projects into northern Gogebic County, so descriptions of some of the area's falls are also included in that chapter.

Before you visit the Porcupine Mountains area we suggest that you first stop at the park's visitors center, just south of M-107 on South Boundary Road. There, a variety of helpful maps show the exact locations of waterfalls within the interior of the park, and park employees can provide up-to-the-minute trail conditions.

132

LITTLE UNION GORGE FALLS

Little Union River, Porcupine Mountains State Park

Although small, Little Union Gorge Falls has a delicate grace all its own. You can almost see the falls from the bridge which spans the small river, and a short walk up the banks brings you to it. The upper part of the falls gradually drops about 30 feet over a long section of dark rocks. The river levels out for about 100 feet, then drops another 15 feet as it slides over slightly angled sections of slate.

Soft, green moss clings to the damp rocks as they rise from the river, and the banks are softly illuminated by sunlight filtered through the surrounding hardwood forest. From both sides, the maple branches stretch to the middle of the small river until they nearly join, and only a thin strip of blue sky shows above the trees.

Directions: From M-107 about 2.5 miles west of Silver City, turn south onto South Boundary Road and go approximately 1.2 miles to the Union River Outpost Campground. Turn left into the campground and go about .3 miles to an iron bridge. Cross the bridge and park on the right. The falls are about 100 feet upstream.

133

TRAP FALLS
(Formerly called Epidote Falls)

Carp River, Porcupine Mountains State Park

Because it is located deep in the interior of the park, anyone attempting to visit this falls should get reliable directions and latest trail conditions at the visitors center.

134

LITTLE IRON FALLS

Little Iron River, Porcupine Mountains State Park

This falls is in the interior section of the park in the White Pine Extension Camp area. Because of its remoteness, anyone attempting to visit this falls should first stop at the visitors center for reliable directions and trail conditions.

135

OVERLOOKED FALLS

136

GREENSTONE FALLS

Little Carp River, Porcupine Mountains State Park

Because of a variety of interesting bridges, walkways and benches built by the DNR, the short trail to Overlooked and Greenstone Falls (and several small falls between them) is one of the most unique and fun that we've walked. Where the easy-to-follow path crosses damp, swampy sections of land, for example, boards have been laid to form walkways. Log bridges—one which has boards nailed across its fattened top, plus a small rope handrail on one side—traverse some areas.

But the most unique feature of this trail, which curves among the towering pines of the Porcupine Mountains, comes when it crosses over the river. The DNR flattened one of the fallen gigantic pines on one side and used it as an 80-foot-long bridge. At both ends, small logs form steps up to the unusual span. But there are no handrails. They really aren't needed because the log is so wide. From that crossing you can get a good view of the gorge—its huge banks of earth towering overhead—that the trail winds through.

At about a quarter mile, the trail reaches beautiful Overlooked Falls. There, the 12-foot-wide stream delicately drops past the moss-fringed rocks which line its banks. In a stream of white against the dark stone, the stream drops about four feet to form a small pool, then arches in two sections around a slab of dry rock in the center. Dappled sunlight spills through the thick branches of lofty pines to highlight sections of the mossy

rock which edges the river. The pines cling tenaciously to the rock border, and here and there send out roots to touch the water.

Less then a mile downstream, the trail approaches Greenstone Falls on a high ridge. Though the path doesn't drop to the riverbanks, the view of the falls from the top of the gorge is beautiful. The Little Carp River here drops about six feet in several sparkling tendrils. A spectacular covering of thick moss on the small stones which line the banks seems to cushion the impact of the water as it glides gracefully over them. The entire area is thickly shaded by towering pines, which allow sunlight to lightly touch only small sections of the velvet moss.

Directions: From M-107 about 2.5 miles west of Silver City turn south onto South Boundary Road and go approximately 18 miles (as the road bears west) to the Little Carp River Road. Turn right (north) onto Little Carp River Road and go .5 miles to a parking area. Do not cross the foot bridge which crosses the river at the parking area, but rather, walk downstream on the near side of the river.

Greenstone Falls

END OF ONTONAGON COUNTY WATERFALLS
IN THE
PORCUPINE MOUNTAINS STATE PARK

137

MINNEWAWA FALLS

Presque Isle River, 4 miles northwest of Tula (Gogebic Co.)

138

NIMIKON FALLS

Presque Isle River, 4 1/2 miles northwest of Tula (Gogebic Co.)

According to Jerry Dennis and Craig Date, authors of *Canoeing Michigan Rivers*, Minnewawa Falls is a series of ledge-drops and chutes that are forced between car- and house-sized boulders to a large pond-size pool at the bottom. Nimikon Falls, according to the pair, is a a 12- to 15-foot drop that all but experienced kayakers should portage around.

We have mentioned their observations because we were unable to find either of the falls by land, although we spent the better part of a day searching for them. Our maps seemed to be accurate but did not include many new roads in the area.

We also encountered other difficulties. Just west of Tula we turned north from M-28 onto USFS-481 but had to stop after about a mile because a bridge was out. From Jack Spur, about three and a quarter miles east of Tula on M-28, we went north on USFS-478. After more than 10 miles of driving through the woods we came to an active logging area, and the road from there was too rough, rutted and rocky to negotiate in our two-wheel-drive truck.

Therefore, even with good, up-to-date maps we would not recommend travel into this area.

5-D

VICTORIA FALLS DAM

West Branch Ontonagon River, 3 Miles south of Rockland

The graceful inward curves of its cement walls, coupled with the still-operating sluiceway, make the Victoria Dam one of the more interesting that we have seen.

If you are in the area to visit the restored townsite of Old Victoria (See page 111 for details), stop at the dam. While in this area you can also search for pieces of copper in the rock piles near the old Victoria Mine site.

Directions: From M-26 just south of Rockland, turn west onto Victoria Road (marked with a sign pointing to Old Victoria). Go approximately four miles on Victoria Road to the townsite of Victoria. Near the Ontonagon River, about halfway between Rockland and Victoria, look for some high-tension wires which cross the road. Under them on a small stream which empties into the Ontonagon on the west side of the road is a miniature un-

named waterfall. To get to the dam, continue past the townsite about one mile to the end of the road.

GOGEBIC COUNTY

In the language of the Chippewa Indians, Gogebic means "where trout rising to the surface make rings on still waters." The persuasive call of the beautiful, untainted natural sights that inspired that graceful phrase centuries ago still lures visitors to this lovely area. More than 315 named lakes and over 1,200 miles of streams lie within the county's borders, and there is an abundance of opportunities for fishing, swimming and boating. Winter sports, particularly skiing and snowmobiling, are also drawing cards to the area.

Over 80 percent of the county's acreage is within the boundaries of the Ottawa National Forest, and most of that land is open to the public.

One of the largest parcels is the 21,000-acre Sylvania Recreation Area, near Watersmeet. To help protect the pristine natural beauty of this tract's clear lakes and streams and lush surrounding forest, motorized traffic on land is prohibited in most areas, and boats with motors are allowed on only two lakes.

Tucked into the corner of this southeastern section of the county is Lac Vieux Desert. During Lincoln's presidency this lake, which is shared with the neighboring state of Wisconsin, was included as part of a reservation and deeded to the Indians. The old village of Katakitckon and a nearby burial ground still remain on the north shore. In ancient times, Lac Vieux Desert marked the beginning of an Indian trail which led north to L'Anse and Keweenaw Bay. If you look closely while traveling US-2 about one mile west of the county line, you can see the trail where it crosses the highway.

Just outside the western edge of the Sylvania tract and also shared with the neighboring state of Wisconsin is the Cisco Chain of Lakes. From Cisco Lake, canoeists can paddle more than 50 miles along paths of connecting lakes which network the area.

Also included in the Ottawa National Forest on the west side of the county is the Black River Valley Recreation Area, which is of particular interest to those looking for waterfalls. In just one two-mile stretch, the main road through the area (the Black River Parkway) passes five easily accessible, beautiful waterfalls. The parkway, which parallels sections of the North Country Hiking Trail along the banks of the Black River, ends at a U.S.F.S. park with beautiful views of Black River Harbor and Lake Superior. Facilities there include a playground and a campground, and a wooden suspension bridge over the harbor leads to the sandy shores of a lovely swimming area.

In addition to the huge federal parcels, the state, too, has set aside land for public use. On the western shore of the Upper Peninsula's largest lake, for example, is a small state park with the same name as the lake—Gogebic. Hiking trails, camping, a myriad of water activities and famed walleye fishing opportunities make this park and lake a popular destination for outdoor enthusiasts. The area has earned a small but unique place in history, too. In 1889 the last stagecoach holdup east of the Mississippi took place just south of Lake Gogebic.

Other state land includes the westernmost tip of the Porcupine Mountains State Park, which projects down into Gogebic County. There, where the Presque Isle River ends its rugged path to Lake Superior, the D.N.R has developed a campground, plus a network of trails which lead to beautiful waterfalls along the river's course.

Where Lake Superior graces the land with her touch, many agate beaches usually line the shore, and Gogebic County is no exception. Little Girls Point, near the westernmost tip of the county, for example, is a good area to wander in search of the elusive stones. Little Girls Point is also fun to visit in the spring, when the area comes alive with smelt dippers.

Gogebic County is not without its man-made attractions. One particularly noticeable addition to the landscape, for example, is the "world's largest Indian," a colorful 52-foot-tall statue of Hiawatha that towers over the county's largest town, Ironwood. For an excellent view of the city, stand next to Hiawatha's moccasins and follow his steadfast and powerful gaze.

Just a few blocks away in the "Old Depot Park" in downtown Ironwood is the Ironwood Historic Museum, which is filled with information and artifacts. Iron mining was an integral part of the city's and county's early history, and there are many abandoned mines in the area.

Today the county bills itself as the "Ski Capital of the Midwest," and for good reason. The county is networked with miles of cross-country ski trails which lead from one beautiful area to another. Downhill skiers are attracted to the four major ski areas that have been built within 14 miles of Ironwood. One, Mt. Zion, on the campus of Gogebic Community College, offers an interesting scenic lookout.

But towering above them all is the famous Copper Peak Ski Flying Hill. Sitting atop the 364-foot summit of Copper Peak, northeast of Ironwood, this 469-foot-long slide is designed to permit ski "flyers" to leap 500 feet and more. It is the only ski-flying hill in the Western Hemisphere, and the annual International Ski Flying competition attracts thousands of sports fans to the area. Many Olympians in training also use the facility to hone their phenomenal skills. During the off-season, visitors can ride an elevator to the top of the man-made structure, which juts 241 feet above the peak. From there the breathtaking view—which stretches out along the horizon to include Wisconsin, Minnesota, Canada, and the ever-present Lake Superior—is especially stunning during fall color.

For more specific information on Gogebic County and its attractions you may contact:

Department of Natural Resources
Wakefield Field Office
Wakefield MI 49968

Forest Supervisor
Ottawa National Forest
US-2 East
Ironwood MI 49938

Ironwood Area Chamber of Commerce
Ironwood MI 49938

Lake Gogebic Chamber of Commerce
Bergland MI 49910

Ottawa National Forest
Bessemer Ranger District
Bessemer MI 49911

Ottawa National Forest
Watersmeet Ranger District
Watersmeet MI 49969

Porcupine Mountains Wilderness State
Park
599 M-107
Ontonagon MI 49953

Upper Peninsula Travel and Recreation
Association
P.O. Box 400
Iron Mountain MI 49938

Watersmeet Chamber of Commerce
Watersmeet MI 49969

Gogebic County

GOGEBIC COUNTY WATERFALLS
LOCATED WITHIN THE

PORCUPINE MOUNTAINS STATE PARK

Several waterfalls, many of them easily accessible, are located within the boundaries of Porcupine Mountains State Park. Following are descriptions of nine—One unnamed falls, plus Manabezho, Manido, Nawadaha, Iagoo, Explorers, Traders, Trappers, and Shining Cloud falls. The largest portion of the park is in Ontonagon County, so descriptions of some of the area's falls are also included in that chapter.

Before you visit the Porcupine Mountains area we suggest that you first stop at the park's visitors center, just south of M-107 on South Boundary Road. There, a variety of helpful maps show the exact locations of waterfalls within the interior of the park, and park employees can provide up-to-the-minute trail conditions.

139
SHINING CLOUD FALLS
Carp River, Porcupine Mountains State Park

140
EXPLORERS FALLS

141
TRADERS FALLS

142
TRAPPERS FALLS
Little Carp River, Porcupine Mountains State Park

These waterfalls are located deep in the interior of the park, and if you want to visit them we suggest that you get direc- tions and current trail conditions at the visitors center.

Manabezho Falls (p. 132)

Manido Falls (p. 132)

Gogebic County

143

UNNAMED FALLS

144

MANABEZHO FALLS
(Also called Presque Isle Falls)

145

MANIDO FALLS

146

NAWADAHA FALLS

Presque Isle River, Porcupine Mountains State Park

This is one of the most beautiful stretches of river we have found in the entire Upper Peninsula. The pristine silence of the forest here is interrupted only by the roar of water, a sound that is never far away. You can take short, easy paths from parking areas along Co. Rd. 519 to each of the falls (see *Directions*) or you can follow more difficult trails along either bank of the river upstream. If you do walk the trails, use great care. The river here is wild, and signs warn of the swift current and dangerous undertows.

The riverbank route begins at the lower parking area, and a short walk leads to a network of stairs which drops to a trail. Just before the trail reaches the river, a side trail branches off to the right. Continue on the wide main path to a suspension bridge and, just above it, a fascinating unnamed falls. The unique beauty of this falls is enchanting, and the brief trip to it is well worth the effort.

There, the force of the powerful river,

as it rushes over its last drop before joining Lake Superior, creates miniature whirlpools along the banks. The spinning action of the water has carved perfect half-circles into the stones which line the bank and polished them to a glossy black. These arcs have also formed in the center of the river, so instead of simply falling over a shelf of rock, the water slips over the circles carved into the stone. The best views of this effect come from the bridge. The forest here draws together on both sides of the river, and branches stretch over the flow.

You could cross the bridge and take a trail along the east bank to the remaining falls, but this trail is rugged and not well groomed. We even found evidence of bear—a pine stump that had been clawed apart to expose a section of fresh wood that contrasted with the old weathered bark that once covered it.

We suggest that you retrace your steps to the side trail and follow that much-

Gogebic County

easier route upstream along the west bank of the river. The narrow path leads about 200 yards through a huge section of pines, which carpet the path with needles, to Manabezho Falls. There, a thick band of white, rushing water, which spans the 150-foot-wide river, drops about 20 feet over a rock shelf. The largest section is tinged with gold, and its heavy flow creates a blanket of foam which trails downstream. The deep-green branches which edge the crest of the falls stretch over the water to hide the banks beneath their thick leaves.

Upstream another 100 yards, Manido Falls drops a total of about 25 feet before settling into rapids. In a mass of white water, the river descends over a network of gradually declining rock steps, then drops over a ledge of stone. From the base of the falls, the water sparkles as it slides over the rough surface of large sections of shale. The riverbanks brush up against small cliffs of rock, and beyond, the towering pines of the Porcupine Mountains are etched against the blue sky. If you look downstream, you can see the beginning of Manabezho Falls. If you look upstream past the thick woods which frame the upper portion of the falls you can see the lace curtain of Nawadaha Falls.

Nawadaha Falls is hard to see from the trail, so you may want to go down the banks to the edge of the river to get a good look at it. The rocks are so thick and the force of the flow so strong here that, as the river drops about 15 feet over a series of rock steps, it creates a blanket of white foaming lace which stretches from the top of the falls to the bottom. Maple and cedar branches extend over the river to frame this jewel of the north woods.

Directions: From M-28, just northeast of Sunday Lake in Wakefield, turn north onto Co. Rd. 519 and go approximately 15 miles to Porcupine Mountains State Park. To see the falls via the short trails from the roadway, proceed as follows: After entering the park continue on Co. Rd. 519 about three miles to a small camper registration building on the right (about a quarter of a mile past the intersection with South Boundary Road). A short walk from directly behind this building leads to Nawadaha Falls.

About a quarter of a mile farther on Co. Rd. 519 is an upper parking area and the start of trails to Manabezho and Manido falls. A few hundred yards farther down is the lower parking area. The path to the Unnamed Falls and the riverbank trails to the other falls begin there.

(Photos, p. 131)

IAGOO FALLS

Presque Isle River, Porcupine Mountains State Park

Iagoo Falls—created as the Presque Isle River slides about six feet over a section of conglomerate rock—is more a large rapids between two smaller rapids than a falls. There is no trail to the falls, but it is close to the road and is worth the short walk through the beautiful woods.

Directions: From M-28, just northeast of Sunday Lake in Wakefield, turn north onto Co. Rd. 519 and go approximately 15 miles to Porcupine Mountains State Park. After entering the park continue on Co. Rd. 519 a little less than two miles (to about a half mile south of South Boundary Road) and park on the side of the road. The river is through the woods on the left (east), and though it is close to the road at this point, you should mark a trail to be safe. When you reach the river, you may have to walk slightly upstream or downstream to reach Iagoo Falls.

(Map, p. 133.)

END OF GOGEBIC COUNTY WATERFALLS
IN THE
PORCUPINE MOUNTAINS STATE PARK

LEPISTO FALLS

Presque Isle River,
1/2 mile south of Porcupine Mountains State Park

As the trail to this falls leaves state park land east of Co. Rd. 519, just north of the park entrance, it is gated and posted, "No Trespassing."

149

NOKOMIS FALLS

Presque Isle River,

2 miles south of Porcupine Mountains State Park

150

ABINODJI FALLS

151

OGIMAKWE FALLS

152

OGIMA FALLS

Copper Creek,
2 miles south of Porcupine Mountains State Park

We do not recommend trying to visit these four falls. All are located in a large tract of private land, and trails to them are almost always blocked by gates.

Chippewa Falls (p. 136)

153

NARROWS FALLS

Black River, 5 1/2 miles north of Bessemer

The Narrow Falls is mainly a rapids, but it is tucked into a very scenic spot on a river that is popular with trout fishermen. The falls is located near the Narrows Spring Campground, and as you start down the trail from the small park you can hear the river below.

Directions: From US-2 in Bessemer turn north onto Co. Rd. 513 (which leads to the Black River Harbor area) and go about 6.8 miles to Narrows Spring Campground, on the right. The falls is located down the hill on the east side of the park. (Map, p. 138)

154

CHIPPEWA FALLS

Black River, 8 miles north of Bessemer

Chippewa Falls is located in one of the most rugged settings we have visited. It is only about a quarter of a mile to the falls from the base of Copper Peak, but there is no trail and the thickly forested terrain descends steeply into a canyon. On a quiet day you can hear the waterfall from the top of the hill.

The 80-foot-wide river gradually drops about 10 feet in several sections over and around huge boulders scattered throughout the streambed. Dead limbs and debris, which extended out from the banks overhead, were strong evidence that the river had risen much higher. Wild, thick woods—the tall, thin spires of pine etched against the azure sky—surrounds the river. Across the river the darkness of the pines encircles a small rounded

meadow whose golden grasses play in the wind. Man could not create a setting as lovely as this.

Directions: From US-2 in Bessemer turn north onto Co. Rd. 513 (which leads to the Black River Harbor area) and go about 8.8 miles to a fork. Take the right fork about a mile to the Copper Peak Ski Hill area. Go just past the gift shop, then turn right and follow the road to the end of the cleared field, which is the landing zone for the ski jumpers. Head straight from the end of the landing zone down to the river. There is no marked trail, so we suggest that you mark a trail (we leave red tags and remove them on the way out) on the difficult quarter-mile walk down to the falls.

(Map, p. 138) (Photo, p. 135)

ALGONQUIN FALLS
Black River, 9 1/2 miles north of Bessemer

Because reliable sources had told us that Algonquin Falls is mainly a rapids, and because there are no marked trails to the falls, we chose not to visit the area. We would not recommend the hike to the inexperienced.

Directions: From US-2 in Bessemer turn north onto Co. Rd. 513 (which leads to the Black River Harbor area) and go about 8.8 miles to a fork. The right fork leads to the Copper Peak Ski Hill area then rejoins Co. Rd. 513 again. Take the left fork to where the roads rejoin, then continue another .3 miles and park on the side of the road. Algonquin Falls is about a half mile from the road on the right (east). (Map, p. 138)

Sandstone Falls (p. 139)

Gogebic County

RAINBOW FALLS

SANDSTONE FALLS

MANIKIKI FALLS

GORGE FALLS
POTAWATOMI FALLS

GREAT
CONGLOMERATE
FALLS

Co. Rd. 513

N

Miles

0   1/2   1

ALGONQUIN FALLS

CHIPPEWA FALLS

6.5 Miles to Bessemer

NARROWS FALLS

156

GREAT CONGLOMERATE FALLS

(Also known as Conglomerate Falls)

Black River, 10 1/2 miles north of Bessemer

157

POTAWATOMI FALLS

158

GORGE FALLS

Black River, 11 miles north of Bessemer

159

SANDSTONE FALLS

Black River 11 1/2 miles north of Bessemer

160

RAINBOW FALLS

Black River, 12 miles north of Bessemer

In the last few miles before Co. Rd. 513 ends at Black River Harbor, short trails—which vary from easy to steep and strenuous—lead east from the paved road through hardwood and hemlock forests to splendid views of five beautiful falls. The trail to Gorge and Potawatomi falls—because of its unusual beauty and unique design, including a series of stairways and observation platforms—has been designated a National Recreation Trail. A segment of the North Country Trail, which winds along the river in this area, also connects the falls.

At about 10.5 miles north of Bessemer the first of these trails leads three quarters of a mile to Great Conglomerate Falls. The trail is wide and smooth, but drops steadily to the riverbank.

There, the river drops in two sections around a large center chunk of conglomerate rock (which gives the falls its name) about 30 feet into a deep gorge. As the two streams descend in several quick stages, the water rushes over the angular rocks and forms small pools before plunging into the base of the gorge. The left section is bridged with logs and assorted debris which trail from the east

(Continued on p. 140)

bank to the bush-topped stone in midstream. This, plus markings on the rocks themselves, suggest that the river has been much higher. From the base, the river moves quickly downstream past heavy boulders which have fallen from the steep walls of the gorge. Farther downstream, the water rushes over these fallen rocks in a small series of rapids before disappearing behind the leafy foliage.

About a half mile farther down Co. Rd. 513 is a double-looped parking area. A very short trail from the north lot leads to Gorge Falls, and an equally brief trail from the south loop ends at Potawatomi Falls. However, we recommend that you take the trail to Potawatomi Falls, then walk along the river (following a beautiful series of fences and platforms) to Gorge Falls.

The two-minute walk along a wide path from the south parking area connects with a series of steps which drops to a trail at the river. To see Potawatomi Falls, bear right, along a wood rail fence which follows the gorge.

Potawatomi Falls is one of the most beautiful on the Black River. The falls itself is at least 40 feet high and drops in two sections around a huge mass of conglomerate stone. As the 70-foot-wide river rushes softly over the conglomerate bed, the clear water catches the sunlight, and each of the small stones interrupts the current to create thousands of sparkles.

Only the slightest bit of water covered the riverbed when we visited, but the falls was still beautiful. The water passed over the rock in small tendrils of white angel hair, which separated and joined in complicated patterns before reaching the base of the gorge. The delicate picture of this falls—nestled in the gorge and surrounded by the deep greens of high summer—is extraordinary.

Less than a quarter of a mile downstream along the fence, an extensive series of stairs rises to a viewing platform above and to the right of Gorge Falls. The water here flows over a mixture of conglomerate stone and smooth bedrock. At the top of the falls, the river narrows to about seven feet wide, then drops past several conglomerate boulders 20 feet into a very steep gorge. The water's pounding pressure fills the base of the falls with golden foam, which contrasts with the reddish tint of the surrounding rocks.

The river shares the path it has cut through the rock with nothing and no one. No trees cover the walls of the gorge, which are sheer and smooth and unable to hold any growth. But tall dark-green pines line the crest of the gorge, and an exquisite blanket of soft, green moss covers the rough mix of stones to near the water's edge.

About a half mile down Co. Rd. 513 from the Potawatomi/Gorge falls parking area, a quarter-mile trail—which includes a few steps roughed in with logs by the forest service—drops very steeply to Sandstone Falls. The forest is not particularly thick here, but the pines, cedars and a scattering of maples and other hardwoods tower overhead.

The falls drops in two sections. The first drop is about five feet through a network of channels the river has gouged out of the sandstone. The water then rushes between two huge conglomerate cliffs, spraying the rock to the right with a fine mist as it drops another 20 feet over a series of sandstone rocks. Upstream, you can see where the river has scooped out hollows in the conglomerate rock. Because the water level was so low, it was possible to study not only the intricate

(Continued on p. 142)

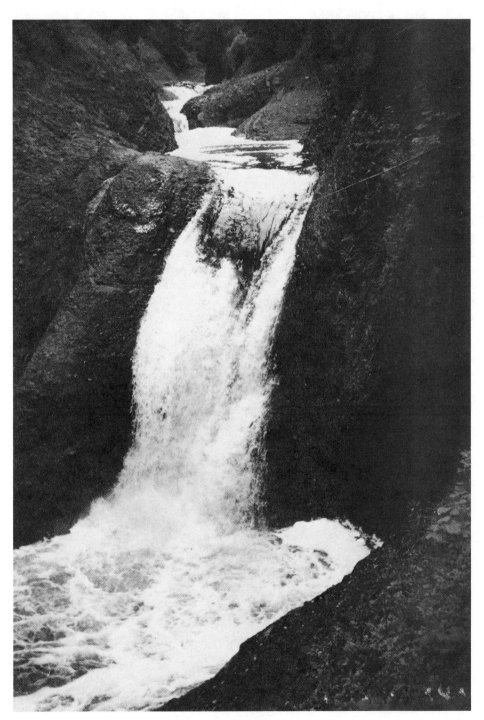

Gorge Falls

Gogebic County

pattern the force of the water has carved into the sandstone along the banks, but also the wildflowers which grow in the tiny crevices.

From the last parking area before the harbor, the trail to Rainbow Falls is the most strenuous. An extensive network of nearly 200 stairs descends very steeply to a platform with views of both the falls and the river upstream.

The 25-foot-wide river here narrows as it flows past huge conglomerate stones on the right. The water then rushes into a small passage between those stones and angular rock cliffs on the opposite bank, makes a sharp turn to the right, and plunges 45 feet over a mass of conglomerate rock into a black pool below. The falling water creates cascading folds of lace as it lightly drops over a huge mass of conglomerate stones in the center. The flow on the right appears to be the strongest, but because of the angle of the viewing platform it is not possible to see the far side of the falls. Foaming waves fill the pool as the force of the water pounds into its blackness. Beautiful red-gold cliffs line the darkness of the pool, and the colored rocks also edge the river as it coasts the rest of the way to Lake Superior.

Directions: From US-2 in Bessemer turn north onto Co. Rd. 513 go about 13 miles to the Conglomerate Falls parking area, on the right (east). The well-marked parking areas for the other four falls are farther north along Co. Rd. 513. All trails are well-marked and well-maintained by the U.S. Forest Service.

(Map, p. 138)

Conglomerate Falls

Potawatomi Falls

161

MANAKIKI FALLS

Maple Creek, 11 miles northeast of Bessemer

The route to Manakiki Falls runs along the top of a ridge on the west bank of the creek about a quarter of a mile upstream to the falls. The path passes over small rolling hills and through partially cleared woods, but across the canyon you can see a much thicker section of forest. There, dark-green pines, interspersed with mature poplar, filter the sunlight to create deep shadows over the wild land. As you approach the falls, the ridge descends to about 25 feet above the river. By the roar of the falls, the strength of the rushing river makes its presence known before you are treated to its visual impact.

As the river begins its run down through this small canyon, in a narrow slash of white water it drops quickly over a shelf of black rock, fans out to a width of three feet, then abruptly plunges through the air into a cool, clear pool 25 feet below. From the pool, the river twists right, at a 90-degree angle, and moves quietly on. Pale-brown sand lines the streambed, and the river brushes up against the sandy banks before continuing its run through the bottom of the canyon.

Directions: From US-2 in Bessemer, turn north onto Co. Rd. 513 and go approximately 13.5 miles (about a half mile past the Potawatomi/Gorge falls parking area) to a gravel road. Turn left (west) onto this road and go approximately three miles to a bridge over Maple Creek. Cross over the bridge, make a *U* turn and park near the bridge. The route to the falls follows the west bank of the river upstream. Although there is no trail to the falls, the quarter-mile walk to it is not too difficult. (Map p. 138)

162

SAXON FALLS
(Also known as Power Dam Falls)

Montreal River, 12 miles northwest of Ironwood

Towering 70-foot-tall cliffs dwarf these half-hidden falls. A dam diverts about 90 percent of the water, and it is difficult to imagine what the falls might look like if normal water flow were resumed. During periods of high water, the beauty of these falls would be reborn.

Directions: From Curry Park in Ironwood, go west on US-2 approximately 9.5 miles to Wisconsin County Road B. Turn right (north) onto Co. Rd. B, and go about 2.3 miles to where Co. Rd B. turns sharply left. Continue straight ahead for a half mile on Saxon Falls Road to its end. Down a hill directly opposite the road end is a power house. Saxon Falls is located just upstream from the power house.

163

SUPERIOR FALLS

Montreal River, 14 miles northwest of Ironwood

A tremendous drop past bordering walls of stone makes Superior Falls a beautiful spot. But like Saxon Falls, most of its water is diverted by a dam upstream, and one can't help but wonder how much more impressive it once was.

The falls alone drops 45 feet, and the total drop, including the rapids upstream, is about 75 feet. At the falls, a network of channels drops over the black rock to cover the lower section of the cliff in a wispy blanket of water before trickling into a small, dark pool below. Soft, golden cliffs rise about 100 feet above the river on the opposite bank, and bushes, which cling precariously to the stone, trail down its face in a *V*.

(Continued on p. 145)

164

INTERSTATE FALLS

(Also known as Peterson Falls and Montreal Falls)

Montreal River, 2 miles northwest of Ironwood

165

UNNAMED FALLS

Montreal River, 1 1/2 miles northwest of Ironwood

A couple of miles northwest of Ironwood, the Montreal River makes a few S-shaped curves, descends a few feet, then turns sharply to the right and plunges 25 feet as Interstate Falls. The water drops over a scattering of rocks into a dark, moderately still pool surrounded by green trees which lean into its blackness. A wall of stone borders the falls on the left, but the remainder of the water's edge is grassy and tree-lined. From the far corner of the large, beautiful pool, the river, hidden by the leaves of the trees, continues on its way.

After our trip to this area we learned that there was an unnamed falls about a half mile upstream from Interstate Falls. You can get to Interstate Falls from either the Michigan or Wisconsin side of the river, and you will see the unnamed falls as you walk the trail along the Wisconsin bank.

Directions: The route to the falls from the Michigan side of the river crosses private property. To obtain permission to visit the falls and get directions, call River Falls Trails (They specialize in guided tours of the area for outdoor enthusiasts.) at (906)–932–5638.

Though we did not do so, it is also possible to visit these falls on the Wisconsin side of the river. You can obtain the Wisconsin directions from either the Ironwood Chamber of Commerce (on US-2 on the eastern edge of Ironwood) or the Hurley Chamber of Commerce (on the main street of downtown Hurley, Wisconsin). (Photo, p. 146)

SUPERIOR FALLS

(Continued from p. 144)

Directions: From Curry Park in Ironwood go west on US-2 approximately 10.8 miles to Wisconsin highway 122. Turn right (north) onto W-122 and go approximatey 4.5 miles to a bridge across the Montreal River. Cross the bridge (you're back in Michigan) and turn left (west) onto the second gravel road. Follow that road to a power station, where there is a road, on the left, with a cable across it. Walk up this old road about 100 feet to the falls, on the right. The falls is located between the power station and a dam about a quarter of a mile upstream. Although a wood fence lines the edge of the cliffs around the viewing area, we would advise caution with children.

(Photo, p. 146)

Superior Falls (p. 145)

Interstate Falls (p. 145)

Gogebic County

POWDER HORN FALLS

Powder Mill Creek, 2 miles northwest of Bessemer

An easy wildflower-lined footpath leads about 250 yards through thick woods to a spectacular view of a deep gorge cut out of the surroundings by Powder Mill Creek.

There, as the river shrinks to a width of only two feet, an upper falls drops about 12 feet over and around small stones that line a narrow corridor in the rock. Wedged into the length of this small chute is a fallen log, its surface wet and green with moss, and the narrow river passes inches beneath it.

The river then widens out to its original 15 feet and drops suddenly over the side of a rock wall. The powerful rush of water swoops down at least 30 feet, and the force of the river forms a beautiful pool to the right of the current. Local young people use this small pool as a summer swimming hole, but the walls of the gorge are so steep that it isn't easy to pick a path to the bottom. Where the river isn't too deep, rocks on the river bed show through the crystal-clear water.

At the side of the falls, wildflowers have taken precarious hold in cracks in the rock, and the deep greens of pine and oak hide the sides of the gorge from summit to the pool's edge. The shadows of many branches, which bend to touch the still waters, stretch over the dark surface.

Directions: From US-2 just after it crosses Powder Mill Creek west of Bessemer, turn right (north) onto Powder Horn Road. Go about two miles to a supper club, on the right. (Powder Horn Road turns to the left at this point.) Park on the right side of the road just before the supper club, then walk back down Powder Horn Road to the second utility pole south of the supper club. Near this pole, you will see the well-traveled path to the falls. You will approach the falls from the top, so use caution.

ROCKY FORTY FALLS

Siemens Creek, 3 miles northwest of Bessemer

Using directions from local residents, we attempted to get to this falls by walking down a set of railroad tracks, then following the stream south. But the area just south of the tracks was very swampy, and we could find no path leading upstream to the falls. We would not recommend travel to this falls.

GABBRO FALLS

Black River, 2 miles north of Ramsay

A few-minutes' walk through a thick hardwood and pine forest scattered with wildflowers ends at the top of a deep gorge. There, the 10-foot-wide Black River makes a slight drop into a small pool, then suddenly plunges beyond the boulders at the edge of the cliff to fall a full 40 feet into the bottom of the gorge. Spray from the main (near) drop rises to the base of the trees at the top of the gorge, while on the far side, small wisps of water escape to run free until joining the main stream at the base of the falls.

These white tendrils contrast with the black wetness of the rock, and the towering pines beyond frame the water in vibrant green.

After this striking drop, the river makes an abrupt turn to the right as it travels along the floor of the gorge. A few feet downstream, the water falls another 10 feet around a huge boulder which rests in the center of the current.

Directions: From the traffic signal in Wakefield go west on US-2 2.2 miles to Blackjack Road. Turn right (north) onto Blackjack Road and go 1.5 miles, following it as it curves sharply left across the Black River. Just after crossing the bridge, turn left and follow the road up a hill (If you continue straight ahead you will enter a ski resort.) A short distance up the hill is a building, on the right. Make a *U* turn and park on the opposite side of the road. The trail begins directly across the road from the building. Because of the deep gorge, it is necessary to view the falls from above rather than at its base, so caution is advised.

NEEPIKON FALLS

Black River, 1 1/2 miles north of Ramsay

Several small drops and rapids extend for hundreds of feet along this section of the Black River, about a half mile upstream from Gabbro Falls. The water was exceptionally low when we visited, which made it difficult to pinpoint exactly which of the many drops was Neepikon Falls. The rapids continue downstream for about 400 yards.

Directions: From the traffic signal in Wakefield go west on US-2 2.2 miles to Blackjack Road. Turn right (north) onto Blackjack Road and go a little less than a mile to a pumping station (Northern Natural Gas Co. Wakefield Plant) on the right (east). In a clearing across the road, follow the pipeline down to the river. Before you reach the river, the trail ends and you must go through some thick underbrush to reach the banks. The falls is located about an eighth of a mile upstream from where the pipeline crosses the river.

Gabbro Falls

GRANITE RAPIDS FALLS

Black River, 3 miles southeast of Bessemer

Just a few feet from a parking area, the 40-foot-wide Black River quickly narrows to 15 feet as it rushes between two huge slabs of granite which reach from shore. Boulders which litter the water in midstream create a rapids as the river drops about five feet, then widens out again. Beyond a few rapids farther downstream, the river turns out of sight.

Bushes and grasses, backed by the green forest, grow right up to the banks of the river, and the shallow, crystal-clear water near the banks makes for excellent trout fishing.

Directions: From US-2 at the traffic signal in downtown Bessemer, turn south onto Moore Street and go .2 miles to First Street. Turn right (west) onto First Street and go one mile to Barber Road. (During this mile, First Street will change to Spring Street, then to Old County Road.) Turn left (south) onto Barber Road and go 1.5 miles to Harding Road. Turn left (east) onto Harding Road and go

1.5 miles to Black River Lane. Turn right (south) onto Black River Lane and go .9 miles to the end of the road. The rapids are on the left.

Granite Rapids Falls

YONDOTA FALLS

Presque Isle River, 4 miles north of Marenisco

A five-minute walk along a short, easy trail ends at the top of Yondota Falls.

The Presque Isle River is close to 30 feet wide here, but it narrows to five feet as it drops about eight feet in a rush through a very narrow gorge that has been carved out of the dark rock. To the right of this small channel, unusual pink traces of color decorate the dark surface of a huge slab of bedrock. Lines, which also mark its surface, suggest that the water level has once risen to cover this rock.

At the end of the chute of water, the river widens, then falls in three sections over and around more of the huge pink-tinged dark boulders. These rocks, which divide the force of the water as it runs past them, are large and dry enough to walk on.

Directions: From US-2/M-64 just west of the Presque Isle River near Marenisco, turn north onto County Road 523 and go three miles to a bridge which crosses the Presque Isle River. Cross the bridge, make a *U* turn and park near a sign, on the west side of the road, that marks the start of the trail to the falls.

A small path on the right bank leads downstream, through thick woods and past wildflowers, to a log archway. Continue beneath the wood arch about 50 feet to the trail's end at the top of the falls.

172

LITTLE GIANT FALLS

Little Giant Creek, 3 miles north of Marenisco

Though this falls is included on most
waterfall lists, we could find no one in
the area who had ever heard of it.

173

JUDSON FALLS
(Also known as Slate River Falls)

Slate River, 1 mile south of Lake Gogebic

174

NELSON CANYON FALLS
(Also known as Marshalls Falls)

Nelson Creek, 1 1/2 miles south of Lake Gogebic

Though both of these falls are located
fairly close to main roads, rangers at
Lake Gogebic State Park told us that
many people have become lost searching
for them.

We made two attempts on foot to locate
these waterfalls but could not reach them.
The large number of logging trails in this
wilderness area made it not only difficult
to use maps, but also nearly impossible
to hike cross-country.

Perhaps since both of these falls are located in the Ottawa National Forest,
someday there will be a marked trail to
them. But for now we recommend that
you heed the rangers' information and do
not attempt a visit to these falls.

KAKABIKA FALLS

Cisco Branch Ontonagon River,
2 1/2 miles southeast of Gogebic Station

An easy-to-follow trail leads 200 yards through the woods to the base of this beautiful, secluded falls.

There, in a 100-yard-long series of drops over shiny black stone, the 20-foot-wide river swiftly descends 40–50 feet. A three-foot-wide gorge, worn into the stone by the current, guides the river down the last drop. Thick, green moss cushions and colors the black rocks, which extend above the water line, and also covers the rock cliffs which rise up from both sides of the river.

Like most streams in this area, the water is copper-colored. Several fallen trees span the river, and the swift flow has also left countless logs and branches washed up against the banks.

Directions: From US-2 approximately 16 miles west of Watersmeet or 12.5 miles east of Marenisco, turn north onto Co. Rd. 527 (marked with a sign) and go about a half mile to a one-lane bridge over the Ontonagon River. Do not cross the bridge, but rather, park on the left side of the road (a sign marks the falls) and follow the trail downstream. Wildflowers and bushes line the beginning of the trail, but then the forest becomes quite thick and fills the air with an ever-present scent of cedar.

176

AJIBIKOKA FALLS

Brush Lake, 5 miles northwest of Watersmeet

Though this falls is located on public land north of County Road 206 in an area near the north end of Brush Lake, there are no marked trails to it. Therefore, we would not recommend visiting this falls.

Gogebic County

MEX·I·MIN·E FALLS

(Also known as Burned Dam Falls)

Middle Branch Ontonagon River, 6 1/2 miles northeast of Watersmeet

During the lumbering heyday in the late 1800s, a dam was built on top of this falls. Logs were held behind the dam until spring, when the gates were opened allowing logs and water to rush to the town of Interior, which had sprung up about six miles downstream. but around 1900 a forest fire destroyed both the town and the dam (the reason for the falls' second name). Today, a sign and a graveyard are all that's left of Interior, and only huge cracked boulders line the edges of the river.

At the falls, the swift flow splashes against those rocks as the 40-foot-wide river drops a total of about 15 feet. First are a few small drops, then the water slides over huge slabs of gently sloping black rock for a total descent of about five feet. Directly downstream, the river rushes over the flat, slightly angled black stone to its largest drop, perhaps seven feet, past both sides of a huge dry-topped boulder in midstream. Beyond this drop, the falls ends in a rush of white water which splashes over small rocks and stones.

Directions: From US-45 in Watersmeet turn east onto Old US-2, also called Co. Rd. 208, and go about 6.2 miles to a gravel road marked by a "Burned Dam Campgrounds" sign. Turn left (north) onto this unnamed road (called USFS-169 on U.S. Forest Service maps) and go 1.1 miles to the entrance to Burned Dam Campground. Turn left into the campground. The trail to the falls is on the left as you enter.

The easy-to-follow dirt trail leads through a predominantly pine forest about 100 feet to the base of the falls.

Mex-I-Min-E Falls

Gogebic County

IRON COUNTY

Iron County's roots reach deep into the iron and lumber industry of the 1800s. The county's mines ran the length of the western section of the Menominee Iron Range, and Crystal Falls was the headquarters of mining in that area.

Of special significance to the lumbering industry is the fact that Iron County is a part of a huge watershed that eventually runs into the Menominee River, a 180-mile-long flow which forms the Upper Peninsula's southern border from the southeast corner of Iron County to Lake Michigan. The Michigamme, the Paint, the Brule, and several other rivers which extend their network of streams and tributaries into the Menominee, formed a perfect path for lumbermen to float their logs to the mills.

Today, this river system is renowned for its fishing, and many anglers try their luck along it and the county's other countless miles of rivers and streams. Lakes, too, abound in Iron County. On the shores of one, First Fortune Lake, is Bewabic State Park, which is an excellent site for water recreation and fishing.

The Iron County Museum, in Caspian, is an excellent place to become more acquainted with the distinctive traits of Iron County, and its unique and enjoyable collection of artifacts from bygone days is well worth a visit. More than 50 major exhibits, dozens of smaller exhibits, and 13 buildings add up to a full afternoon's excursion, especially for those interested in the mining and lumber industries. Included in the museum park are homes of the county's early pioneers as well as displays of pioneer life during the early chapters of the county's history.

For more specific information about Iron County and its attractions you may contact:

Department of Natural Resources
District 2 Office
P.O. Box 300
Crystal Falls MI 49920

Iron County Chamber of Commerce
Iron River Branch Office
1 East Genesee Street
Iron River MI 49935

Ottawa National Forest
Iron River District Ranger
Iron River MI 49935

Upper Peninsula Travel and Recreation
Association
P.O. Box 400
Iron Mountain MI 49801

SNAKE RAPIDS

Net River, 8 miles west of Amasa

West of Amasa, the 50-foot-wide Net River narrows to form Snake Rapids. At the base of the quarter-mile-long rapids, the river widens out again to a near lake-sized 200 feet. There, towering pines on the far shore are reflected in the clear, copper-tinged water. Angling opportunities promise to be excellent, and the shallow rapids make them an ideal spot for fishermen with waders. Facilities at a state-forest campground, near the base of the rapids include several secluded campsites, pit toilets and a boat ramp.

The trail to the rapids involves a five-minute walk along an overgrown and long-forgotten dirt road to the river. From there the trail follows the riverbank upstream about a quarter of a mile. Heavy underbrush surrounds the riverbank path, and the air is thick with the enticing smell of the large cedars that line the route. Here and there, wildflowers poke through the fresh green ferns that carpet the forest floor.

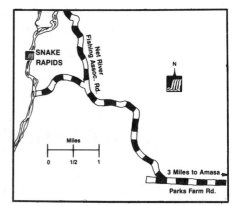

Directions: From US-141 just south of Amasa, turn west onto Parks Farm Road (called West Pine Street on the east side of US-141) and go 3.3 miles to a fork. Take the right (north) fork and follow the public access signs about 2.5 miles to another fork. Take the left fork and continue to follow the public-access signs about 1.4 miles to a campground at the river. The rapids are about a quarter of a mile upstream.

CHIPMUNK FALLS

Net River, 6 miles northwest of Amasa

The land on both sides of the river at the falls is privately owned.

180

MARGESON FALLS

Margeson Creek, 11 miles northeast of Crystal Falls

Though this falls is located on state
land, all access roads that we found were
on posted private property.

181

LOWER HEMLOCK RAPIDS

182

HEMLOCK RAPIDS

Paint River, 3 miles southwest of Amasa

Routes to both rapids cross private
property, so we were unable to reach
them.

183

CHICAGON FALLS

Chicagon Creek, 6 miles northwest of Crystal Falls

The best views of this falls come from
an easily accessible small island.

To get to it you must navigate the twists
and turns of a trail which passes through
a thickly wooded oak, birch and poplar
forest. Wildflowers and blackberry bram-
bles cover the ground, and as the trail
nears the falls, you can smell the huge
cedars which line the river. The trail
breaks out of the forest at the top of the
falls, where a little stream jogs to the
right around a small island. The trail

crosses this stream to the island and
views of the falls from its head.

The 25-foot-wide river drops about
three feet, then turns to the left and
swiftly slides 20 feet down a flat chute of
rock. After foaming over huge black
boulders in the middle of the current, the
river falls again, about five feet, then set-
tles down to skate over rocks and cedar
roots as it widens out farther downstream.

(Continued on p. 159)

CHICAGON FALLS

(Continued from p. 158)

Directions: Go west of Bewabic State Park on US-2 for .6 miles to the Long Lake access road (marked with a sign). Turn right (north) onto this good gravel road and go about two miles to the public access, on the left. Continue straight another half mile and, as the road turns left (west) around the end of Long Lake, look for a two-track trail (marked with two steel posts) on the right.

Turn right (north) onto the two-track and go past two turns, the first to the left, the second to the right. At the second turn we pulled off the main trail and parked on a seldom-used trail to the left. The route to the falls continues down the main (right) trail for about five minutes to a trail which branches off to the left. Take that left trail a very short distance to just past a large washout, bear right and go about 200 yards to a trail which branches off to the left. Follow that left trail a short distance to the falls.

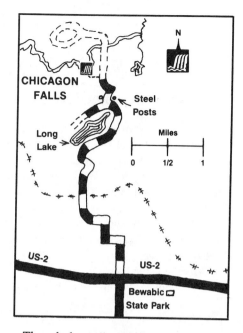

Though these directions sound involved and complicated, this one-mile route is very easy to follow. Nevertheless, we marked each turn with a red ribbon to secure our return route.

Glidden Rapids (p. 160)

Iron County

GLIDDEN RAPIDS

Michigamme River, 6 miles southeast of Crystal Falls

There is no trail to this small rapids, which drop only about a foot, and the route to them requires a rough 20-minute trek through the forest. During normal or high-water conditions, the river would probably swallow up this rapids. We visited during a dry spring, when the river was low, and that is probably the only reason they were visible.

Directions: Go east of Crystal Falls on M-69 about 5.2 miles to the Michi-gamme River. Cross the river and park on the right (south) side of M-69. To reach the rapids walk a half mile downstream on the east bank. The first 100 yards is through a low-lying swampy area, but after crossing a few small creeks, the terrain climbs steeply to the top of a hill. Continue walking along this hill for 15 minutes and the rapids will be around the first bend in the river after the hill. (Photo, p. 159)

HORSERACE RAPIDS

Paint River, 8 miles southeast of Crystal Falls

Once, according to local legend, a lumberman either deliberately or accidentally rode a log down the length of Horserace Rapids. The Paint River was used to float logs to the mills, and as the man worked to break up a log jam, as the story goes, it broke loose and he was carried along with it. Tales like that, plus spectacular natural beauty, make Horserace Rapids a very appealing stop.

(Continued on p. 161)

HORSERACE RAPIDS
(Continued from p. 160)

The road to the falls ends on a bluff, and a short walk down the steep rock-strewn hillside ends at a scattering of huge pines and cedars that reach high above the river.

But an 80-foot-high bluff on the opposite side of the river towers over even those majestic trees and fills the sky with its dark presence. One of the most striking features of this bluff is an unusual almost aqua-colored moss which is scattered over its surface. This light aqua-green mixes with the darker greens and browns of the forest to create a beautiful display of changing hues.

In the river below, Horserace Rapids rushes over huge, sharp rocks that have tumbled from the banks. The rapids stretch for hundreds of yards down the 30-foot-wide river. When we visited, the water level was lower than usual, but in the past it has been high enough to float logs.

Not far away, on the Menominee River in Dickinson County, is another Hor-serace Rapids. That falls, the first to be named, has been swallowed up by the backwaters of the Hydraulic Falls Dam.

Directions: Go approximately seven miles south of Crystal Falls on US-2 to Horserace Rapids Road, just before the Joseph Caspary Roadside Park. (A sign just before this intersection points to the Iron County Airport and Horserace Rapids Road.) Turn left (east) onto the blacktopped road and go 1.7 miles to the junction with Airport Road. Turn right (south) and continue on Horserace Rapids Road .7 miles to the Horserace Rapids parking area.

Horserace Rapids

IRON COUNTY DAM SITES

6-D
LITTLE BULL FALLS DAM
Paint River, 6 miles southeast of Crystal Falls

There is no waterfall remaining at this site, which is called Public Recreation Area #22.

Directions: Go about five miles east of Crystal Falls on M-69 to Lake Mary Road. Turn right (south) onto Lake Mary Road and go 3.6 miles to Little Bull Road. Turn right (west) onto Little Bull Road and go one mile to a fork. Take the right fork one mile to the dam site.

7-D
BRULE ISLAND FALLS DAM
Brule River, 11 1/2 miles southeast of Crystal Falls

There are no waterfalls at this dam site, which is surrounded by private property. This site may be reached by going north on Chapin Street out of Florence, Wisconsin.

8-D
MICHIGAMME FALLS DAM
(Also known as Lower Michigamme Falls)
Michigamme River, 10 miles southeast of Crystal Falls

There is no waterfall remaining at this site, which is called Recreation Area #8. Facilities there include a boat ramp and pit toilets.

Directions: Go east out of Crystal Falls on M-69 about 5.2 miles to the Michigamme River. Cross the river and continue east another 4.5 miles to Camp 5 Road. Turn right (south) onto Camp Five Road and go approximately 9.7 miles to Lower Dam Road. Turn right (west) onto Lower Dam Road and go 2.7 miles to the dam site.

9-D

PEAVY FALLS DAM
(Also known as Upper Michigamme Falls)
Michigamme River, 9 miles southeast of Crystal Falls

There is no waterfall remaining at this site, which is called Public Recreation Site #9.

Directions: Go east out of Crystal Falls on M-69 about 5.2 miles to the Michigamme River. Cross the river and continue east on M-95 another 4.5 miles to Camp 5 Road. Turn right (south) onto Camp 5 Road and go approximately seven miles to Upper Dam Road. Turn right (west) onto Upper Dam Road and go 2.4 miles to the dam site.

10-D

HEMLOCK FALLS DAM
Michigamme River, 6 miles northeast of Crystal Falls

There is no waterfall remaining at the site of the dam.

Directions: Go 4.2 miles east of Crystal Falls on M-69 to a blacktop road (A sign just before the intersection reads, "Mansfield Location"). Turn left (north) onto the unnamed road and go about 2.5 miles (after 1.5 miles the road becomes Old M-69 Road) to where it turns to the right and meets the Michigamme River. Do not cross the river, but rather turn left at a sign which commemorates the Mansfield Mine disaster (many miners were killed when the Michigamme River broke into the mine) and go 1.5 miles to the dam site.

DICKINSON, MENOMINEE AND DELTA COUNTIES

Bordered by Wisconsin on the west and the beautiful Green Bay of Lake Michigan on the east, Delta, Menominee and Dickinson counties form the southernmost tip of the Upper Peninsula. Because of the small number of waterfalls in each of these counties, we've combined them into one chapter.

As in the rest of the U.P., countless outdoor pursuits are available in this tri-county area. Thousands of acres have been set aside for public enjoyment in the Hiawatha National Forest and the Copper Country, Escanaba River, and Lake Superior state forests. Their many lakes, streams and forests have been visited by generations of serious hunters and fishermen.

One of the most popular and beautiful rivers in the area is the Menominee, which winds its way along the western border of Dickinson and Menominee counties to form the Michigan/Wisconsin state line. Thick woods and steep, rocky cliffs surround the wide, swiftly flowing river. The Menominee, once famous for the abundant whitefish and sturgeon in its deep-blue waters, now offers good walleye fishing opportunities, especially in the backwaters of its dams.

In Menominee County long before roads were built, the extensive river system served as the main mode of travel throughout the area. Those who used the waters left a rich historical heritage, and it is easy to fill several days investigating this county's past. Ancient native Americans used the waterway to travel to the copper pits in the Keweenaw Peninsula and on Isle Royale. The southern portion of the river was home to the Menominee Indians, who played a large part in the area's history. As Europeans spread throughout the area, the river was used to remove timber harvests and as a route in the search for fortunes in minerals hidden beneath the earth.

One of those minerals, iron ore, has also played an important role in the history of Dickinson County. The Eastern Menominee Iron Range stretches through the county, and several abandoned mine sites in the area which are open to the public provide a fascinating glimpse into the past. One of the most interesting remnants of the mining era is the Cornish Pumping Engine, the largest steam engine ever built in North America. The 50-foot-high pump, which may be visited in Iron Mountain, was used to remove water from the Chapin Mine, the area's most productive iron mine. Another landmark in Dickinson County is the Pine Mountain Ski Jump, near Iron Mountain. Well-known for its annual mid-February tournaments, Pine Mountain is, at 932 feet, the longest ski jump in the world.

Bordering Lake Michigan northeast of Menominee County is Delta County, whose highways are major crossroads for Upper Peninsula travelers. The proximity to Lake Michigan originally opened up the county to industrial interests, and it's largest city, the port of Escanaba, is still a major shipping point for iron ore from mines to the north. The city is also the permanent site of the Upper Peninsula State Fair, which is held annually in August.

Directly east of Escanaba, across both Little and Big Bay De Noc, is one of Michigan's most fascinating ghost towns. Located on the west side of the aptly named Garden Peninsula, which juts into Lake Michigan to form Big Bay De Noc, the town of Fayette was originally established in 1867 by Fayette Brown as the site of a smelting operation for the Jackson Iron Company. but the area's hardwoods, which are needed for the smelting process, gradually were depleted, and in 1891, after producing nearly 230,000 tons of pig-iron, the company abandoned Fayette.

During the 1960s the State of Michigan purchased the area and turned it into one of our most beautiful state parks. The town is situated on the shores of Snail Shell Harbor, a beautiful natural cove formed by a high limestone bluff to its north and a small strip of land to its south. Pretty and unusual stones cover the shoreline, which makes the walk to a campground south of the townsite especially beautiful. Several of the original buildings have been restored, complete with furnishings of the period, and parts of the old kilns and the main smelting building are still standing. A very informative interpretive center has been added. It's easy to spend many hours here, and as you walk through the once-bustling town, you can't escape the eerie sensation that it is in a state of suspended animation, just waiting for an opportunity to come alive again.

Another natural attraction in the area that you won't want to miss is Kitch-iti-ki-pi (Big Spring), located in Palms Book State Park in Schoolcraft County. This 300-foot-long, 75-foot-wide, 40-foot-deep elliptical pond is Michigan's largest spring, and it is beautiful. The best way to enjoy it is by taking a self-propelled raft across the water, which is as clear as glass. As you glide quietly over the pond, through a hole in the center of the raft you can see trees laying silently on the sandy bottom, the tendrils of the moss which covers them drifting slowly back and forth in the current. If you look closely, you can even see huge rainbow trout that hide beneath the fallen logs. And at the very bottom of the bowl, if the light is just right, it is possible to catch a glimpse of the sand which billows out in small puffs from the action of the spring beneath the earth's surface.

For more specific information about these three counties and their attractions you may contact:

Delta County Area Chamber of
Commerce
Escanaba MI 49829

Department of Natural Resources
District 3 Office
Box 495
Escanaba MI 49829

Department of Natural Resources
Felch Field Office
Felch MI 49831

Department of Natural Resources
Norway Field Office
P.O. Box 126
Norway MI 49870

Menominee County Chamber of
Commerce
Menominee MI 49858

Upper Peninsula Travel and Recreation
Association
P.O. Box 400
Iron Mountain MI 49801

DICKINSON COUNTY WATERFALLS

186

MILL POND FALLS
Sundholm Creek, 1 mile southwest of Felch

Though the falls is located just south of the Swedish Lutheran Church, about one mile southwest of Felch, it cannot be reached from there without crossing private property. The approach from the southeast involves a compass- and map-guided trek across state land. We would not advise visiting this falls without first obtaining directions from the D.N.R. Field Office in Felch.

187

HORSERACE RAPIDS
Menominee River, 1 mile south of East Kingsford

Horserace Rapids is located in the backwaters of Hydraulic Dam, and is visible only during periods of low water. During two visits to this area, we saw no sign of a rapids.

Fumee Falls

FUMEE FALLS

Fumee Creek, 3 1/2 miles northwest of Norway

On the north edge of the Helen Z. Lien Roadside Park, Fumee Creek makes a few drops, forms a small pool, then falls 25 feet over the side of a limestone bluff, which looms out from towering cedars and pines. As the water falls it forms two small streams, which glide over and around dark, moss-covered rocks. These stones are particularly interesting because, unlike the smooth, softly rounded stones found at most waterfalls, they have yet to succumb to the water's persistent erosion and are sharply angled and rough-surfaced.

From the base of the falls, fallen rocks stretch down a hill to a small footbridge, which spans the five-foot-wide creek. You can glimpse this falls from your car, and a short walk will take you to the water's edge. A small short trail leads to the top of the bluff.

Directions: Go almost four miles west of Norway on US-2 to the Helen Z. Lien Roadside Park, on the north side of the highway. (Map, p. 169)

LITTLE QUINNESEC FALLS
(Also known as Kimberly Clark Falls)

Menominee River, 4 miles southwest of Norway

The land on the Michigan side of this falls is privately owned, and there are no good views from the Wisconsin side. From the Kimberly Clark plant, which stretches along the river in Niagara, Wisconsin, it is possible to get a partial view of the falls as it runs over the black rocks near the right edge of the factory.

Directions: Go south from Norway on US-8 and cross the Menominee River into Wisconsin. Continue on US-8 for approximately three more miles as it bears west to US-141. Turn right (north) onto US-141 and go about three miles to the town of Niagara. As you drive through Niagara, you will see the Menominee River, about a block away on the right. Drive down any of the streets that lead to the street that follows next to the river, turn left and go until you see the large paper mill on the right. Park in a large truck lot, on the right just before reaching the mill. The falls is upstream about 400 yards, but there is no access across the private property. (Map, p. 169)

Piers Gorge Area, Menominee River

190
UNNAMED FALLS

191
MISICOT FALLS

Menominee River, 2 1/2 miles southwest of Norway

192
SAND PORTAGE FALLS

Menominee River, 3 miles southwest of Norway

In the Piers Gorge Scenic Area, just south of Norway, the beautiful Menominee River drops four times. Not all of these falls are named or shown on maps, but they can be easily seen by following a smooth, clear trail through the hardwood forest. This area once was referred to as the Great Sand Portage, because Indians used to carry their canoes from the base of the unnamed falls to the upper end of Sand Portage Falls. Legend has it that the variegated rock, which composes most of the trail, has been worn smooth by the countless mocassins which have tread the ground during those portages.

The trail begins by crossing through a cedar swamp, so common to the U.P., and as it passes beneath the fragrant boughs, it crosses two foot bridges. Just after crossing the second bridge, through the trees on the left is an unnamed falls, which drops about a foot in a golden band of color across the entire river.

From there the trail climbs over a few stones and roots up the face of a rock hill, but the path is still easy. From the crest of the hill, crowned with huge oaks and pines, you can see the river clearly. On the left is the second falls which, similar to the first, is more like a rapids, with short drops continuing for several feet.

The trail continues down to the right, and when we visited in May, a riot of trillium formed a snowy backdrop to the deep browns and greens of the forest. The trail descends through the towering trees back to the river and, on the left, Misicot Falls. The trail is still about 70 feet above the water, and the view is encompassing.

Past the treetops you can see the swift, dangerous current as it rushes across the rocks, then foams over the five-foot drop of the main falls. The 150-foot-wide river narrows drastically as it passes over the falls, and the black water rolls up toward the sky as it sweeps over a large boulder in the middle of the flow. The river then continues in a cascade of small rapids.

Just downstream from the falls, you can see that this area is aptly named. There, the strength of the Menominee River has cut through the rock to form a 60-foot-deep gorge. The walls of this gorge jut out from the shore just past the falls, and as the river curves around the steep rock face, the stone wall takes the full force of the water. Eventually it, too, will wear away.

The trail continues upstream and, about 30 minutes from Misicot Falls, passes beneath a power line. Take the next trail to the left, and as you turn through the woods you can hear Sand Portage Falls. The short walk ends at the edge of a 30-foot-high cliff with excellent views of the river and the falls. The river splits around a small island, and as it narrows where the two flows rejoin, Sand Portage Falls begins. Similar to both unnamed falls,

this is more like a rapids, but it has a larger and longer drop than either of the unnamed falls.

The Piers Gorge Scenic Area was one of the loveliest in this part of the state in terms of the nature and wildlife it afforded. During our early morning visit, we saw several ducks, frogs and dozens of deer tracks. Silver squirrels ran through the leaves, a walleye was pulled from the waters, and we heard the haunting call of Canadian geese as they flew swiftly up the river, following its every turn.

Directions: From Norway go south on US-8 about a mile and a half to Piers Gorge Road, which is the last road before crossing the Menominee River. Turn right (west) onto Piers Gorge Road and go about a half mile to a fork. Take the left fork and follow the gravel road one mile to the parking area and the start of the trail.   (Photos, p. 171 and 83)

DICKINSON COUNTY DAM SITES

11-D

Twin Falls Dam
Menominee River

There is no waterfall at this site, located near Iron Mountain about four miles north of US-2 on Co. Rd. 607.

12-D

Ford Falls Dam
Menominee River

There is no waterfall at this site, located near Kingsford on Cowboy Lake Road, off Woodward Avenue.

13-D

Hydraulic Falls Dam
(Also known as Big Quinnesec Falls)
Menominee River

There is no visible waterfall at this site. *Directions*: From US-141 in East Kingsford turn west onto Brietung Road and go one mile to Hydraulic Falls Dam Road. Turn left (south) onto that road and go .3 miles to the dam.

14-D

Sturgeon Falls Dam
Menominee River

Water spills over a small section of the dam, but there is no natural waterfall at this site.

Directions: From Co. Rd. 577 about 2.5 miles south of Vulcan, turn west onto Power Dam Road and go about a half mile to the dam.

15-D

Power Dam Falls
Sturgeon River

There is no waterfall at this site.

Directions: Go north out of Loretto on Co. Rd. 573 and turn right (east) onto the first gravel road. Continue east to the second gravel road on the left. Turn left (north) and follow this road to the dam.

Misicot Falls (p. 168)

MENOMINEE COUNTY WATERFALLS

193

QUIVER FALLS

Menominee River, 3 1/2 miles southwest of Faithorn

Because the Michigan side is private property, Quiver Falls must be viewed from the Wisconsin banks of the Menominee River.

A small island divides the river here, and a set of rapids flows 200–300 yards on each side of it before joining again. The bigger drop is on the Wisconsin side. The water also swirls softly around log pilings, which stretch up from the river as an eerie reminder of what once must have been an old wooden dam or railroad bridge.

Directions: Cross over the Menominee River south of Norway on US-8 into Wis-consin and go about three miles to US-141. Turn left (south) onto US-141 and go about 8.5 miles to Kremlin Road. Turn left (east) onto Kremlin Road and go about nine miles to the uninhabited village of Kremlin. From the intersection of three roads in Kremlin, continue straight and cross a set of railroad tracks. Just after crossing the tracks, the road forks. Take the left fork (the right fork is blocked by a large sand bank) and follow it about a mile as it winds to a parking area near the river. A short trail from the parking area leads to the river, and the falls is about a quarter of a mile up-stream.

PEMENE FALLS

Menominee River, 6 miles south of Faithorn

Down some steps only about 70 feet from a parking area is uniquely beautiful Pemene Falls. The falls is more like a rapids as the river drops about seven feet in a 100-yard strip. The thick forest here spreads toward the edge of the river but is halted by sheets of rough, black rocks, which gradually creep from under the surface of the water, then angle sharply upward to pave the banks. The rock is slippery even above the water, evidence that the river level fluctuates. A few cement abutments indicate that the area may once have been dammed.

Directions: From Faithorn go south about 8.5 miles on Co. Rd. 577 to Co. Rd. 374. Turn right (west) onto Co. Rd. 374. and go about three miles to the last sand road before crossing a bridge on the Menominee River. (Just before this intersection is a D.N.R. public-access sign on the right.) Turn right (north) onto the sand road and go a half mile to the Jerry Welling Site •

From there, you can see the falls upstream, but to reach them you must continue north about another half mile to a trail road that heads left into the woods. That trail leads .1 mile to the parking lot area at the falls.

DELTA COUNTY WATERFALLS

195

CHANDLER FALLS

Unnamed Stream, 6 miles north of Escanaba

We were informed by D.N.R. officials in Escanaba that, because of a dam, this falls, located about two miles southeast of Carrol Corners, is under water and no longer visible.

196

HUNTERS BROOK FALLS

Hunters Brook, 16 miles northeast of Escanaba

This falls—which, according to local residents, is located near where Hunters Brook empties into the Escanaba River—is on private property.

RAPID RIVER FALLS

Rapid River, 7 miles north of Rapid River

Because of its easy access in a large, grassy park, Rapid River Falls is a popular stopping place.

The river, here, is about 40 feet wide, and the falls spans it as a copper-tinted ribbon of water. Four tiers, spread several feet apart, drop a total of 12 feet before the river rushes past the park on its left bank. Smooth limestone slabs, similar to those at Whitefish Falls (see page 26), border the banks to make a smooth, easy trail. The river rushes swiftly between the stone borders, which hold back the trees somewhat.

All in all, this is a very pleasant park to enjoy a family picnic or just to stop for a few minutes and visit the falls. Children, too, will enjoy the playground and the river nearby. Facilities at the large park include picnic tables, barbeque pits and a flowing well.

Directions: Go 6.5 miles north of Rapid River on US-41 to S-15 Road, the last road before crossing the Rapid River. Turn left (west) onto S-15 Road and go .3 miles to the park and falls.

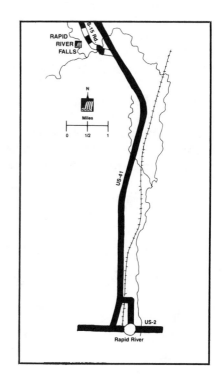

HAYMEADOW FALLS

Haymeadow Creek, 9 miles northeast of Rapid River

The walk to Haymeadow Falls is a lovely 10-minute trip along a marked trail through a thick hardwood forest, over rolling hills and past tiny streams to Haymeadow Creek.

There, in a copper-colored band, the 15-foot-wide falls drops about three feet, then foams up over fallen rocks at its base before continuing down the river. A lush cedar and birch forest touches the riverbanks, and a fallen tree spans the creek below the falls. A bridge, which crosses the stream at the base of the falls, is a perfect spot for picture-taking.

In the back of our minds as we traveled through the backwoods of northern Michigan, we always hoped for a glimpse of large animals, such as deer or perhaps

(Continued on p. 177)

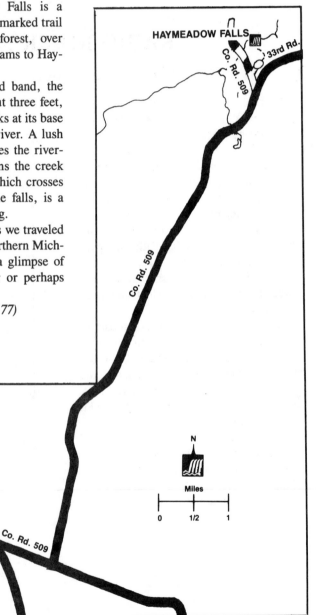

Delta County

HAYMEADOW FALLS
(Continued from p. 176)

even a rare bear. Near the bottom of our mental wildlife list were smaller animals.

But that changed at Haymeadow Falls. As we gazed at the falls, we saw a splash of water followed by a silver, glistening object which hurled itself from the base of the falls. A salmon had tried to leap the falls. It brought to mind the wonders that had gone unseen beneath the flows and drops we had visited. We see only the beauty of the falls and the peaceful drifting of the river, but the beauty continues below the surface and is there for all who would care to notice.

Directions: From the blinker light on the east side of Rapid River, go about two miles east on US-2 to where it bears south at Co. Rd. 509. Continue straight (east) on Co. Rd. 509, go about a half mile, and turn left (the road is still Co. Rd. 509). Go north on Co. Rd. 509 about eight miles to a fork. The paved right fork is 33rd Road (also called Co. Rd. 442). Take the gravel left fork, which is Co. Rd. 509, about an eighth of a mile to Haymeadow Campground, marked with a sign on the right. The trail to the falls begins at the northeast corner of the campgrounds. About 150 feet after you start down the old four-wheel-drive trail, a walking trail branches left to the falls. Although this path is marked by a small sign, it is very easy to miss.

A second trail to the falls begins at a parking area, on the right about a quarter of a mile past the campgrounds on Co. Rd. 509.

DELTA COUNTY DAM SITES

16-D

BONEY FALLS DAM
Escanaba River

Directions: Go seven miles north of Cornell on Co. Rd. 523 to a set of limestone pillars on the right and a sign that reads, "Escanaba Power Dam #4 Boney Falls." This is the entrance to the dam.

LOWER PENINSULA WATERFALLS

199

OCQUEOC FALLS

Ocqueoc River, 9 miles east of Onaway

As the Lower Peninsula's only named waterfall, Ocqueoc Falls certainly deserves to be included in this collection. Located in a secluded section of woodland, this falls is a beautiful addition to any trip to the area, and its charm shouldn't be missed.

Less than 100 feet from a parking area, the Ocqueoc River makes three drops for a total of about 10 feet. As the water

sweeps over the smooth shelves of black rock, the falls forms snow-white accents between each level section of the river.

A mixture of hardwoods surrounds the falls, and a few dark-green pines are scattered along the banks. As you walk through a thick layer of dried oak leaves, which have covered the earth since the previous autumn, the only sounds that pierce the silence are the leaves rustling underfoot and the muted roar of the river hidden beyond the trees. As you approach the river, the trails of light-brown leaves dwindle, and a few fall into the rushing water.

Directions: Go approximately six miles east of Onaway on M-68 to Ocqueoc Road. Turn left (north) onto Ocqueoc Road and go about 2.8 miles to Ocqueoc Falls Highway. Turn right (east) onto Ocqueoc Falls Highway and go approximately 1.5 miles to the Ocqueoc River. Cross the river and turn left, into the parking area. The trail to the falls heads west, through a small picnic area, about 100 feet to the falls.

Ocqueoc Falls

APPENDIX I

WATERFALLS
THAT MAY BE VIEWED
FROM A CAR

NAME OF WATERFALL	NUMBER	PAGE
Alger Falls	16	18
Eagle River Falls	103	104
Fumee Falls	188	167
Haven Falls	110	109
Jacobs Falls	104	105
Lower Huron Falls (partially seen)	56	58
Rapid River Falls	197	175
Reany Falls (partially seen)	43	45
Scott Falls	18	21
Warner Falls	30	34

APPENDIX II

ALPHABETICAL LISTING
OF WATERFALLS
BY ALL KNOWN NAMES

Many waterfalls in this book have been known or are presently known by more than one name. Following is a listing of all the known names of every waterfall and dam site in this book.

NAME OF WATERFALL	NUMBER	PAGE	NAME OF WATERFALL	NUMBER	PAGE
Abinodji Falls	150	135	Bushy Creek Falls	45	46
Agate Falls	111	112	Canyon Falls	82	78
Ajibikoka Falls	176	153	Caps Creek Falls	34	39
Alder Falls	46	48	Carp River Falls,	40	42
Alger Falls	16	18	SW of Marquette		
Algonquin Falls	155	137	Carp River Falls,	37	41
Au Train Falls	21	24	W of Marquette		
Bacco Falls	82	78	Cascade Falls	123	117
Baltimore Falls	120	117	Cataract Escanaba	1-D	55
Big Eric's Falls	56	58	Falls		
Big Falls	58	62	Chandler Falls	195	174
Big Quinnesec	13-D	170	Chapel Falls	7	10
Falls			Chicagon Falls	183	158
Black Point	1	3	Chipmunk Falls	4	7
Rapids			(Alger Co.)		
Black River Falls	33	38	Chipmunk Falls	179	157
Black Slate Falls	64	65	(Iron Co.)		
Bonanza Falls	130	121	Chippewa Falls	154	136
Bond Falls	112	113	Chocolay Falls	25	30
Boney Falls Dam	16-D	177	Cliff Falls	50	52
Bridalveil Falls	10	12	Conglomerate Falls	156	139
Brule Island Falls			Copper Falls	105	105
Dam	7-D	162	Dault's Falls	76	76
Burned Dam Falls	177	154			

(Continued on p. 182)

(Continued on p. 184)